Praise for

MATURITY MATTERS®

There is one word that is foremost in my mind in these days, and that word is "discipleship." Bob Dukes and his team are engaged ministry partners at New Hope. Together, we have been implementing and prototyping many of the discipleship processes in *Maturity Matters;* and we are seeing lives changed! These incredible leaders, and the truth they teach, are invaluable assets as we witness our church grow, our members restored and disciples becoming mature men and women of God. Bob's book provides the insights and practical steps for helping people, and churches, take the next major step in building disciples.

> **—Rev. Rhys Stenner,** Senior Pastor, New Hope Church (GA)

Bob Dukes' new book speaks into the issues of the "maturity deficit" we are seeing today within the Western Church, where current culture and thinking takes precedent over the plumb line of the Word of God. Bob, with his incredible experience at WDA and his passion for discipleship, takes us through a well-tried and tested pathway. As you would expect from WDA and Bob, there is an abundance of resources throughout the book, giving the Body every opportunity to grow into maturity and be more aware of the promises of God.

> —Sr. Executive with Operation Mobilization (name withheld for security purposes)

D1430692

Bob Dukes discipled me nearly forty years ago. His life and words still impact my ministry today. *Maturity Matters* explains what a master-discipler has learned over four decades. You will learn the "how" in addition to the "what" and "why" of discipleship.

—**Dr. Rocky Ramsey,** Senior Pastor Corryton Church (TN)

In *Maturity Matters,* Bob Dukes clearly defines the insidious declination and historical relevance of the church's perceived value in today's society. But, he doesn't leave the reader stuck in the dilemma…he provides both strategy and tactics to solve the problem at a grass roots level. I laud Bob Dukes for taking a complex subject and making it concise, understandable and easy to apply through a linear path from Philosophy all the way to Prototypes. Throughout *Maturity Matters* the reader will conclude that the solution is credible and it provides a path he or she CAN and will WANT to follow. You will truly be taken on an exciting journey!

—**Ross Greene,** Founder and CEO, Greene Consulting Associates

The impact of WDA on my life was first realized during my college days over 30 years ago, before I knew God would bring us back together when I became a pastor. In our discipleship program, we equip and minister to hundreds of adults every week. WDA's *Restoring Your Heart, Getting Started, Foundations* and *Life Coaching* components are cornerstones of our weekly discipleship ministry. The effectiveness of WDA's progressive model is a construct allowing the equipping of God's people to be far more than a content only experience. Our weekly adult discipleship numbers have continued to grow during this season, but more importantly –

our people are growing and becoming mature disciples of our living Lord!

My wife, Mary Lynn and I have had the privilege of knowing Bob and Linda Dukes and their family for over thirty-five years. We have taken the discipleship principles of WDA's Ministry and applied them practically in our own lives as well as in our church setting. These Jesus-modeled principles and practices work not only here in America, but also in our short-term international mission efforts. In both places we have seen remarkable maturity in those we've discipled. Wherever we are, Christlike maturity matters to God (Col. 1:28-29).

MATURITY MATTERS®

The Priority and Process for Disciple Building in the Church

BOB DUKES

WDA®
Disciple Building

Maturity Matters®:
The Priority and Process for Disciple Building in the Church

Book Design by Cara Stein / BookCompletion.com

NOTE:
In the interest of editorial brevity and simplicity, these documents treat gender-neutral and gender-plural references with the masculine pronoun "he" rather than "she," "he or she" or other constructions. When clarity is better served by other words, we follow whatever usage seems to aid readers best. Worldwide Discipleship Association follows Scripture in joyfully recognizing that God created man and woman in His image as equal recipients of His grace and mercy.

Table of Contents

Foreword

We are created to glorify God, to love Him, and to enjoy Him forever. Though our forebearers chose to go their own way, thereby breaking communion with their Creator and bringing death to the human race, that did not change the reason we are made. God loves us, and in the fullness of time, He came in His incarnate Son to accept the judgment over sin on the cross. Then, showing His invincible power, Jesus rose from the grave. Now, by His grace, all who come to Christ in true repentance and faith are made over again; they are "being transformed" into the likeness of Him who gave Himself for us (2 Cor. 3:18b, ESV).

The full scope of what this means staggers our imagination. To think that in our relationship with the Son of God, we are members of His "household" (Eph. 2:19) and "heirs of God and fellow-heirs with Christ" (Rom. 8:17). Does not just the thought bring a smile to your face? Wonderful as is your future inheritance, try to count your present experiences of God's blessings every day: delivered from "the domain of darkness" that once held you captive (Col. 1:13), "set free in Christ Jesus from the law of sin and death" (Rom. 8:2), and "cleansed" on the inside "by the washing of water with the word" (Eph. 5:26b). But you soon discover there is much more, that His blessings cannot be numbered. "No eye has seen, nor ear heard, nor the heart of man imagined, what God has prepared for those who love him" (1 Cor. 2:9).

To sum it up, look at Jesus. He is the photograph of the person God is recreating you to be. If you could only grasp "the breadth and length and height and depth" of "the love of Christ" (Eph. 3:18, 19), you would have glimpses of what you are becoming. But you must follow Him. In receiving Christ, you enroll in His school of discipleship, a curriculum that requires active faith, which translates into obedience. Paul compared it to the discipline of an athlete training for a race. Anything that does not contribute to winning the prize has to be laid aside, and he adds: "Let those of us who are mature think this way" (Phil. 3: 15a; cf. 1 Cor. 9:24-27). In another context, he exhorts the church to grow up in Christ, "until we all attain to the unity of the faith and of the knowledge of the son of God, to mature manhood" (Eph. 4:13a).

In this life, I expect most of us have a lot of growing up to do. There is so much more to learn. For myself, I can resonate with Paul's yearning to know more about sharing in the "sufferings" of Christ, "becoming like him in his death" (Phil. 3:10). This is heavy stuff, though not surprising. Did not Jesus tell His disciples to "take up his cross daily" and follow Him (Luke 9:23; cf. Matt. 10:35)? I confess that I have more to learn regarding the practical application of this teaching. The same pertains to many other areas of my immaturity.

Thankfully, God is not finished with any of us yet! He wants to lead us into dimensions of His glory that we have not even dreamed of. Yes, the journey will probably go through adversity, and our faith will be sorely tried. But whatever the hardships, Jesus promises to be with us, even to the end of the age (cf. Matt. 28:19). The beautiful thing is that God works through every circumstance to conform us more perfectly to the image of our Lord.

Maturing in Christ describes the way saints are made. That is why I appreciate this book. It comes to grips with the maturity deficit, underlying the spiritual poverty and ineffectual witness characterizing much of the modern church, especially in the Western world. More importantly, the book charts a course to deal with the problem, offering constructive ways to disciple people in the lifestyle of the Great Commission and equip them for works of ministry.

The author's own experience in making reproducing disciples gives his writing a ring of authority. For many years, Bob Dukes has been training people for spiritual leadership following the pattern of Jesus with His disciples. He has a shepherd's heart. And as you read these pages you will feel his deep love for Christ and His church. His message is clear. It is down-to-earth. If you take it to heart, you will know why maturity matters to God, to the praise of His glory.

Dr. Robert Coleman
Distinguished Senior Professor of Evangelism and Discipleship
Gordon-Conwell Theological Seminary

Introduction

Not long ago, I had coffee with an old acquaintance. It had been years since we'd seen each other. We first met while our children were active in the same church youth group. We co-hosted sleepovers, car-pooled to retreats, and even co-vacuumed popcorn from the youth room carpet. As he sipped a latte, he reminisced, "Those were fun times, but now that the kids are grown, I've stopped going to church."

Sensing my confusion, he went on to say that after decades of faithful attendance, he wasn't leaving a particular church. Instead, he was leaving church altogether.

"I'm sure it's great for some people, but it never worked for me. It seemed like all the church leaders wanted me to do was show up, pay up, and shut up." He added, "I'm tired of playing that game."

The sad truth? He's not alone. Recent surveys reveal that most churches are either losing members or membership is not keeping pace with population growth. [1] As my friend put it, "Those church leaders never really cared about my family or me. They just wanted me to care about them, their programs, their agendas, their budgets, and their building campaigns. Now, many of those buildings are sitting empty."

I understand his frustration and confusion, but I disagree with my friend's conclusion. I meet often with church leaders from a variety of traditions. Most show deep concern for their flocks and agonize over the best ways to address needs. The current problems stem not from lack of concern or commitment. The underlying issue is about a lack of discipleship. According to one survey among reformed and evangelical pastors, eighty-one percent said there was "no regular discipleship program or effective effort of mentoring their people or teaching them to deepen their Christian formation at their church." [2]

Today's church leaders know how to teach the Scriptures, but they often don't know how to help people like my friend grow to maturity. Unfortunately, immature people are self-centered. They can only see the world from their own narrow perspective. They fail to see the challenges and obstacles others face. And when things don't go their way, they take their Bibles and go to another church—or, like my friend, stay home.

As we mature, we are transformed.

And sadly, church leaders often give up hope of seeing parishioners grow to maturity. John Ortberg tells the story of a church member who exhibited immature behavior most of his adult life. "He was once a cranky young guy, and he grew up to be a cranky old man. But even more troubling than his lack of change was the fact that *nobody was surprised by it*. It was as if everyone simply expected that his soul would remain withered and sour year after year, decade after decade. No one seemed bothered by the condition. It was not an anomaly that caused head-scratching bewilderment. No church consultants were called in. No emergency meetings were held to probe the case of this person who followed the church's general guidelines for spiritual life and yet was nontransformed." [3]

As we mature, we are transformed. We develop the capacity to see others' needs and display the courage and wisdom to help them—even if it means sacrifice and suffering. God demonstrated this type of love for us, and it's also what He expects from us.

Jesus summed it up by saying, "This is My command: love each other" (John 15:17). And later, "Greater love has no one than this: to lay down one's life for one's friends" (John 15:13). Even among Christians, that sort of love is hard to find.

In his enduring passage on the superiority of love, the Apostle Paul links the capacity to love others to an adult (mature) perspective:

"Love is patient, love is kind. It does not envy, it does not boast, it is not proud. It does not dishonor others, it is not self-seeking, it is not easily angered, it keeps no record of wrongs. Love does not delight in evil but rejoices with the truth. It always protects, always trusts, always hopes, always perseveres... When I was a child, I talked like a child, I thought like a child, I reasoned like a child. When I became a man [mature], I put the ways of childhood behind me" (1 Cor. 13:4-7, 11).

The Scriptures clearly teach that believers need to be trained and equipped to grow up—to become more and more like Christ and able to love as He loved. Paul urged young Timothy and the other leaders in Ephesus to keep this in mind as they discipled their fellow believers:

"As I urged you when I went into Macedonia, stay there in Ephesus so that you may command certain people not to teach false doctrines any longer or to devote themselves to myths and endless genealogies. Such things promote controversial speculations rather than advancing God's work—

which is by faith. The goal of this command is love, which comes from a pure heart and a good conscience and a sincere faith" (1 Tim. 1:3-5).

"So Christ himself gave the apostles, the prophets, the evangelists, the pastors and teachers, to equip his people for works of service, so that the body of Christ may be built up until we all reach unity in the faith and in the knowledge of the Son of God and *become mature*, attaining to the whole measure of the fullness of Christ. Then we will *no longer be infants*, tossed back and forth by the waves, and blown here and there by every wind of teaching and by the cunning and craftiness of people in their deceitful scheming. Instead, *speaking the truth in love, we will grow to become in every respect the mature body of him who is the head*, that is, Christ." (Eph. 4:11-15, emphases added)

My friend's been a Christian since high school, but he still needs to grow to maturity. If he does, he'll develop a better understanding of how the kingdom of God functions. He'll recognize his need to remain committed to and involved with a community of believers.

As we address the matter of immaturity in the church, more believers will grow in the faith and knowledge of God.

As we address the matter of immaturity in the church, more believers will grow in the faith and knowledge of God. And as the church becomes filled with mature Christ-followers, we'll do a better job of addressing the issues in the surrounding culture. After all, Christians are "the light of the world" (Matt. 5:14) and "the salt of the earth" (Matt. 5:13). But if we want all these things to occur, church leaders also need to make some changes.

Unless believers grow to maturity we tend to become more like the Pharisees than like Christ. Ortberg warns, "The great danger that arises when we don't experience authentic transformation is that we settle for what might be called pseudo-transformation. We know that as Christians we are called to 'come out and be separate,' that our faith and spiritual commitment should make us different somehow. But if we are not marked by greater and greater amounts of love and joy, we will inevitably look for substitute ways of distinguishing ourselves from those who are not Christians. This deep pattern is almost inescapable for religious people: If we do not become changed from the inside-out – if we don't morph – we will be tempted to find external methods to satisfy our need to feel that we're different from those outside the faith." [4] According to one survey this *"pseudo-transformation"* characterizes most Christians in America and explains the problem many non-believers have with the church. [5]

If we don't morph – we will be tempted to find external methods to satisfy our need.

For decades, Worldwide Discipleship Association (WDA) focused on discipling college students. Our staff poured their lives into young men and women to help them apply biblical truth. We're grateful most of our alumni are walking with Christ and providing spiritual leadership in their homes and churches. But after graduation, they share a common lament: "Our local church doesn't seem to know how to help people grow to maturity. Can you help?"

After sensing the Lord's prompting, we launched The 28/20 Project, an effort to help local church leaders teach people to put Christ's commands into practice. Its name came from what the church calls The Great Commission, our Lord's charge to discipleship in Matthew 28:20a, "And teaching them to obey everything I have commanded you."

As we began the project, we knew we'd heard from the Lord because we experienced a sudden, dramatic increase in spiritual warfare. In spite of the fierce opposition, we knew God had taught us many truths that will help local churches facilitate maturity. Our plan of action looked like this:

- We began with a maturity **philosophy**. We knew Jesus had a plan for building mature leaders. His Great Commission assumed this "pattern of sound teaching" (2 Tim. 1:13), and the early church employed it to help people grow in Christlikeness. Of course His plan would apply to the contemporary church, as well.

- Using Jesus' approach as a template, we designed a **process** for producing maturity in the church that included a progressive, intentional architecture for growth.

- Building on this process, we developed practical **programs** to support maturity. These can be implemented in local churches through lay leaders.

- Next, we produced a progressive **curriculum** that provides the content and training needed to support the programs.

- Finally, we built partnership **prototypes** in a few local churches that have implemented our process.

This book represents an explanation and overview of what we've learned so far. We've reached a critical intersection. Christians need to be trained to think, feel, and act like Jesus (Luke 6:40).

God commands this for the glory of His name. In addition, our culture has a desperate need for mature people.

This project is much larger than our small organization. It will require collaboration and cooperation among all believers, especially Christian leaders. The declining Western Church needs restoration. The Church in other nations needs to be better equipped. If we hope to achieve these goals and follow Christ's commands, we must work together.

The maturation process may seem daunting and uninviting. After all, we don't like it when someone says, "Grow up!" But living a mature life of service to others is essential. Remember the last time you encountered that rude driver or the over-zealous rival fan? What about the surly shopkeeper or the mud-slinging politician?

We know maturity is important. But we don't always understand the best way to harness the processes that produce it.

We know maturity is important. But we don't always understand the best way to harness the processes that produce it. If you're a church leader who feels this way, you're not alone. In this book, we'll present practical, biblical approaches for producing maturity. As you read and study this material, we hope you'll grow—and join a movement that urges others to do the same.

Everybody needs to grow and mature, but this book is aimed at Christians who realize something has gone terribly wrong in the Western societies that once embraced biblical Christianity. These believers sense, even suspect, that underlying issues exist within the church that connect to the cultural decay and the shift of worldviews.

And they're right. God has placed the church—along with the family—at the center of the maturation process. By strengthening the church, we bolster the family and, in turn, our society.

Our enemy understands this. That's why, in our postmodern culture, all these institutions find themselves under siege. We need mature leaders who will stand against the evil one and retake lost territory in our homes and churches.

I believe God is allowing time for Western cultures to repent, or at least time for His Church to prepare for hardship and increasing persecution. But since time is short and precious, we must act wisely.

Most Christian leaders lead busy lives. That's why we designed this book to be read in a few hours, providing an overview of core concepts. The Epilogue shares an invitation to join an ongoing conversation about implementing the suggested programs. The information-packed Appendix will meet the needs of those who want still more information. If you want to learn even more, we hope you'll contact us.

Today, many believers hope and pray for an outpouring of God's grace and mercy to yield a worldwide spiritual awakening. I join them in asking God to bring into churches the kind of revival that spills into the surrounding culture.

But while we wait and pray, we can also act by installing processes and programs that produce maturity. And we don't need to choose between prayer and action. As Scripture reminds us, "The horse is made ready for the day of battle, but the victory rests with the Lord" (Prov. 21:31; cf. 1 Cor. 3:6).

The solution to the widespread immaturity found among believers today is achievable, but not simple.

The solution to the widespread immaturity found among believers today is achievable, but not simple. A clear display of God's sovereign rule in the hearts and lives of His followers requires wisdom and knowledge, a realignment of priorities, and an application of Kingdom principles.

Leaders must understand, balance, and apply all the dynamics that contribute to progressive growth and sanctification. This requires both a strong faith and a new focus. As we fix our eyes on things unseen, the outcome will be a deeper faith, drawn in part from church leaders who consistently equip believers. As we help them put truth into practice, faith grows. The rewards are both temporal and eternal.

Unfortunately, some church leaders don't invest the necessary effort to "equip his people for works of service" (Eph. 4:12). Others have their own leadership agenda, one that doesn't include maturity.

When Christ returns, He will hold all leaders accountable for their stewardship. That will spell blessing for some and embarrassment (or worse) for others.

But many leaders have made a commitment to honor Christ by helping His people grow to maturity. These men and women have "ears to hear" (Mark 4:9). They'll discover and implement maturation processes within their local churches that produce Christlike followers. They'll celebrate the traditions that support such growth and help change any that don't.

To accomplish this maturity-minded goal, wise leaders are willing to embrace the challenge of intense spiritual warfare. I'm praying God will sound His trumpet of restoration in these dark days, calling people to "rebuild the ancient ruins and restore the places long devastated" (Isa. 61:4).

I hope you're one of those He calls. May His grace and power rest upon you for the glory of His name.

Chapter 1

The Priority and Benefits of Maturity

We face a growing cultural crisis due to a breakdown of the processes that produce maturity.

The Apollo Project of the National Aeronautics and Space Administration was a stunning success. It accomplished what no one thought possible: putting the first men on the moon. In fact, the project was so successful that stellar missions became the norm. And no one anticipated what lay ahead.

The thirteenth Apollo mission became the unfortunate exception. One disaster after another plagued its astronauts until their safe return seemed impossible. The support team in Houston became discouraged to the point of despair. In the movie *Apollo 13*, one character voiced the thought on everyone's mind: "This could be the worst disaster NASA's ever faced."

The response of the Lead Flight Director (played by Ed Harris), who saw the situation from a different perspective, has become part of film lore. "With all due respect, sir, I believe this is gonna be our finest hour." Courageous, committed leaders initiated a heroic team effort that beat the odds, won the heart of America, and reverberated around the world.

Western civilization, once a fortress of spiritual strength, faces a growing crisis as we witness the breakdown of character and morals. Amid the selfish individualism fueled by a consumer-oriented society, families have fragmented. Schools have exchanged a biblical value base for a naturalistic worldview supported by secular humanistic philosophies and evolution. Cultural icons tout immorality and greed. Government seems confused, unsure if a foundation of absolutes exists on which to establish law and policy.

Career politicians have displaced statesmen. And if that isn't enough, the popular media seems bent on destroying what remains of a biblical worldview. Even church leaders vie for control and market share. Many choose the limelight over foot-washing and a remodel over transformational discipleship. To add to the stress, radical Islam threatens the eradication of Western society. And then there's the nightly news and its evidence of ever-increasing violence in our streets. But underlying the crisis in society is a crisis of maturity.

But underlying the crisis in society is a crisis of maturity.

An old adage, said to have come from political philosopher and historian Alexis de Tocqueville, suggests that "America is great, because America is good." The quote goes on to affirm that the secret to America's goodness lies in a population imbued with and supported by biblical spiritualism. [6]

Regardless of the source, the principle comes straight from Scripture. The goodness (maturity) of the Church does have a profound impact on the preservation of its society and of the world as a whole. The most profound Statesman the world has ever known asserted that mature believers are indeed "the salt of the earth" (Matt. 5:13) and "the light of the world" (Matt. 5:14).

In His Sermon on the Mount, Jesus laid the foundation stones of His Kingdom. He promised an inner transformation of the heart for those who would follow Him. That transformation would produce an obedience that superseded the written code. Christ urged wise men to put His truth into practice like a man who builds his house on a rock (Matt. 7:24). But He also warned of the consequences when people didn't obey Him, when the salt "loses its saltiness" (Matt. 5:13b).

The modern church is rapidly losing its influence in culture and stands in danger of being "trampled underfoot" (Matt. 5:13c).

The modern church is rapidly losing its saltiness in culture and stands in danger of being "trampled underfoot" (Matt. 5:13c). Many in the emerging generation consider it largely irrelevant, and it faces increased persecution from a society that calls good evil and evil good (Matt. 5:20).

Dallas Willard suggested this has occurred because Christians failed to apply the teachings of Christ. And the consequences, he said, are profound.

More than any other single thing, in any case, the practical irrelevance of actual obedience to Christ accounts for the weakened effect of Christianity in the world today, with its increasing tendency to emphasize political and social action as the primary way to serve God. It also accounts for the practical irrelevance of Christian faith to individual character development and overall personal sanity and well-being. [7]

The failure of churches to teach people to put the truth of Christ into practice has contributed to the maturity deficit that exists today. But this crisis didn't develop overnight. A gradual erosion of character has taken place in both the church and the culture at large.

Without mature leaders of character, societies ultimately decline and eventually fail altogether. We shouldn't be surprised when secular institutions reject absolute truth and embrace temporal values. But tragically, many churches and church institutions have abandoned a biblical worldview as well. Others have neglected spiritual nurture for programs in which success is determined primarily (if not exclusively) by numbers of participants, effectively sacrificing maturity for mere attendance.

Ironically, we live in a society filled with spiritual needs but increasingly hostile toward Christianity.

Ironically, we live in a society filled with spiritual needs but increasingly hostile toward Christianity. Worse still, the name of God is dishonored and His glory tarnished in a culture where pollsters report that a majority of Americans claim to be Christians, but fail to live as Christ lived. [8] Studies reveal little difference in lifestyle statistics such as divorce rates between nominal church members and the general population, but couples "who generally take their faith seriously, living not as perfect disciples, but serious disciples enjoy significantly lower divorce rates than mere church members, the general public, and unbelievers." [9]

But many church-goers seem to be searching for some elusive commodity that will satisfy their spiritual hunger. In some communities, a revolving-door syndrome exists in which people move from church to church on a hunt to fulfill deep spiritual longing.

Across the country, the number of mega-churches continues to increase as smaller churches close their doors. [10] Is this a healthy trend? It may be too early to tell, but in our zeal to attract outsiders, we may have encouraged self-centeredness instead. Many of today's churchgoers show up with a consumer mentality, expecting to get something rather than expecting to be challenged to lay down their lives to follow Christ.

God's Will and Growth to Maturity

Developing a process for growth that produces maturity is a big order. But since God commands it, we can expect Him to provide the wisdom we need to accomplish the task. In fact, the process of discovery both develops character and leads to more significant leadership responsibility. Scripture hints at this dynamic: "It is the glory of God to conceal a matter; to search out a matter is the glory of kings" (Prov. 25:2).

The Kingdom of God reserves a high place for humanity, the only element of creation made in God's image. But to inherit His Kingdom, fallen humankind must be redeemed. The redemptive process involves three distinct yet integrated components. Keeping them in balance allows us to celebrate what God has accomplished in Christ, see the importance of growth to maturity, appropriate God's grace wisely, and remain hopeful as we live holy lives in a fallen world. The following overview helps us maintain a proper perspective. As followers of Christ:

1. **We are justified,** *already saved* from the penalty of sin. Jesus came to justify us by His substitutionary death and give us forgiveness of sins so we can be accepted as children of

God. We repented of our rebellion and placed our faith in His sovereign goodness and grace. And our holy God not only forgave us but credited us with His righteousness.

2. **We are being sanctified,** *being saved* from the power of sin. Christ came to be the lord of our lives. Through the power of the Holy Spirit, He delivers us from Satan's grasp, reshapes us in His image, and enables us to love and address the needs of a fallen humanity by sacrificial service. We extend His reign into this world. In the process, He transforms our hearts and helps us grow to maturity, gradually changing our character and conduct into His likeness.

3. **We will be glorified,** *saved* from the presence of sin. One day, Christ will return in power and glory, deliver us from all evil, transform us, and rebuild this fallen world into a new one where righteousness dwells.

Historical Developments

During the Reformation, Protestant Christianity recovered the doctrines of a grace-based justification. They rejected the tradition of justification by works and replaced it with the doctrine of justification by faith alone. The Bible became the new cornerstone for orthodoxy, and *"Sola Scriptura!"* ("By Scripture alone") replaced many of the traditions and teachings of the medieval church.

As the good news of justification by faith in Christ's atonement spread throughout Northern Europe, it changed political landscapes, freed hearts from guilt and uncertainty, and broke the shackles of the church's spiritual domination. These sweeping changes heralded a new age and a new hope.

By separating justification from works of righteousness, the Reformers made one position clear: the doctrine of salvation by works was rightly rejected. Some historians say Luther even wanted to remove the book of James from the New Testament canon because of its emphasis on works of righteousness as evidence of true faith. [11]

The doctrine of sanctification toward maturity, however, proved a greater challenge. Sanctification should produce good works, but these works are fruits of justification, not a prerequisite to it. With a few noteworthy exceptions, the Reformers failed to forge a unified, biblical humanism that clarified how people could attain spiritual maturity. [12]

Instead of reforming the church, most neo-classical thinkers wanted to enthrone a new deity: Man.

To further complicate matters, the Renaissance emerged in Southern Europe as a counter-weight to the Reformation. Instead of reforming the church, most neo-classical thinkers wanted to enthrone a new deity: Man. Weary of church oppression and buoyed by a new optimism, Renaissance thinking gained traction throughout Europe. Eventually, Cartesian philosophy led to rationalism, and reason replaced the revelation of Scripture as the new basis for truth.

Once Darwinism came into vogue in the twentieth century, man (the peak of the evolutionary process) emerged as the supreme deity. A new religion, secular humanism, replaced theocracy.

Secular humanists rejected scriptural authority and many other biblical doctrines but championed concerns linked to man's development. Socialism, human rights, ecology, psychology / soul-care, personal development, justice, concern for the poor, and similar causes became rallying points. Universities offered new disciplines, and old disciplines offered new curricula to support these humanistic concerns.

Even theology wasn't spared. Resonating with many (but not all) of Christ's teachings, liberal theologians embraced a new social gospel. They focused on the teachings of a humanitarian Christ but downplayed His deity. Jesus did teach that we should live mature lives, loving our neighbors; but He also taught that in order to do so, we need redemption from sin. He alone can secure justification and sanctification.

More and more often, conservative theologians and churchmen found themselves on the defensive. But instead of countering the secularist movement with a biblically balanced, Christocentric humanism, they reacted. Many conservative Christians placed less emphasis on issues related to human development on earth and focused instead on the message of forgiveness of sin (justification) and the coming reign of Christ (glorification). Evangelical conservatives neglected biblical sanctification. Liberal humanists, however, popularized it—in a new, non-Christ-centered form.

This has led to a situation where many who profess Christ fail to reach maturity.

Sadly, growth to maturity never fully reemerged as a priority among evangelicals. This has led to a situation where many who profess Christ fail to reach maturity. Rather than growing to spiritual adulthood, they live defeated lives. They're ensnared by old habits and patterns of sin, unable to embrace the joys of knowing God. Incomplete or inadequate approaches to sanctification have replaced sound teaching and doctrine. Consequently, cults and false teachers plague these immature spiritual sheep like parasites.

This is in part what John Piper urges when he says:

Justification is not an end in itself. Neither is the forgiveness of sins or the imputation of righteousness. Neither is escape from hell or entrance into heaven or freedom from disease or liberation from bondage or eternal life or justice or mercy or the beauties of a pain-free world. None of these facets of the gospel diamond is the chief good or highest goal of the gospel. Only one thing is: seeing and savoring God himself, *being changed into the image of his Son so that more and more we delight in and display God's infinite beauty and worth."* (emphasis added) [13]

But let's be honest. Most current approaches for helping Christians grow to maturity aren't working. Many church leaders realize something is wrong but don't know how to correct the problem. A shift may have started, but old traditions persist. Alister McGrath recognizes that we need a better strategy.

Evangelicals have done a superb job of evangelizing people, bringing them to a saving knowledge of Jesus Christ as Savior and Lord, but they are failing to provide believers with approaches to living that keep them going and growing in spiritual relationship with Him... Many start the life of faith with great enthusiasm, only to discover themselves in difficulty shortly afterward. Their high hopes and good intentions seem to fade away. People need support to keep them going when enthusiasm fades. [14]

I'm convinced that most church leaders are sincere, zealous followers of Christ, committed to helping people grow in Him. They've given their lives to Christ and His agenda. The problem doesn't lie with their passion for God. Instead, it comes from their failure to have a strategic plan that produces maturity and has a practical use in their church.

We need a new approach, a new perspective. Any new approach requires a new way of thinking. And that's a challenge in itself. It also requires biblical balance because the growth process involves both mystery and method. God's in charge, but He expects us to do our part.

God is building a people for His own pleasure who are able to rise above the world, take on His characteristics, and live significant lives that impact all eternity. But like the courageous mission leader of *The Apollo 13 Project*, we need a proper perspective of His plans and strategies in order to fully apply His process.

Fulfilling The Great Commission

A friend tells the story of two groundskeepers. After one dug a hole, the other filled it up. A puzzled bystander approached them for an explanation for this bizarre behavior.

"It's simple," came the answer. "The guy who *plants* the trees is sick today!"

This corny story illustrates the current state of affairs in much of Christian ministry. Hard work, diligence, and organization aren't enough. We've left out an important component of our mission.

At the end of His ministry on earth, Jesus said, "Therefore go and make disciples of all nations, baptizing them in the name of the Father and of the Son and of and the Holy Spirit and *teaching them to observe everything I commanded you.* And surely I am with you always, to the very end of the age" (Matt. 28:18-20, emphasis added).

The Commission to extend Christ's Kingdom throughout the earth is more than an evangelistic mandate. It also includes the training (discipling, equipping, nurturing) of believers to apply all the teachings of Christ. And in the process, growth to maturity will take place.

The modern church must appreciate and apply the specifics of our Lord's commands. His Commission to equip mature followers extends to today's church leaders and includes two key concepts:

- A mandate to teach a complete, definitive body of truth to all believers

- A mandate to teach the application of this truth

The Priority of Helping People Grow to Maturity

During the period of commissioning His church leaders, Jesus reminded Peter that sacrificial care for His sheep was the trademark of true leadership and evidence of true love for Him (John 21). I wonder if Ezekiel's rebuke of Israel's unfaithful shepherds (Ezek. 34:1-10) was the underlying context.

Jesus reminded Peter that sacrificial care for His sheep was the trademark of true leadership and evidence of true love for Him.

Either way, Jesus made His point: In the newly-formed church, leadership meant caring discipleship. So, are modern church leaders caring for the Lord's sheep? Do we protect and equip our fellow believers, help them grow to maturity, or use them to support selfish ambitions?

Only God knows hearts. But some leaders appear to be more concerned with other agenda items (even those promoted in Scripture) than helping people grow to maturity. The problem seems to be an issue of neglect more than blatant disobedience. But as my friend Pastor Rhys Stenner reminds me, "Partial obedience is still disobedience."

The Blessings of Maturity

"What's in it for me?" has become part of our social fabric in a world where most people look out for number one. Scripture, however, exhorts us to lay down our lives for others (Phil. 2:1-5).

Is it wrong, then, to want to know how a particular activity might benefit us before we participate? Scripture admonishes us to "Put off your old self, which is being corrupted by its deceitful desires; to be made new in the attitude of your minds; and to put on the new self, created to be like God in true righteousness and holiness" (Eph. 4: 22-24). But doesn't the Bible also say to "Love your neighbor as you love yourself" (Matt. 19:19)?

At first, the notion of considering personal benefit may appear to contradict the sacrificial life Scripture encourages. After all, Jesus gave up His life on the cross and then urged us to follow His example by taking up our cross. But we must remember that the Bible also says it was "For the joy set before Him, He endured the cross, scorning its shame" (Heb. 12:2).

The benefit of joy motivated our Lord to finish His mission. This sense of balanced tension seems to be what Jesus meant when He said, "For whoever wants to save their life will lose it, but whoever loses their life for me *will find it*. What good will it be for someone to gain the whole world, yet *forfeit their soul*?" (Matt. 16:25-26, emphases added)

Christ assumes that the longing for true life will move us to deny ourselves all the lesser pleasures and comforts of life.

John Piper places this tension in biblical perspective, "In essence, Jesus says that when you "deny yourself" for His sake and the gospel, you are denying yourself a lesser good for a greater good. In other words, Jesus wants us to think about sacrifice in a way that rules out self-pity. This is, in fact, just what the texts on self-denial teach. He assumes that the longing for true life will move us to deny ourselves all the lesser pleasures and comforts of life.

The measure of our longing for life is the amount of comfort we are willing to give up to get it." [15]

As long as our approach is Christ-centered and faith-supported, we can be both self-sacrificing and self-preserving at the same time. The benefits are biblical, eternal, and accompanied by godly maturity. Paul summed it up by saying, "Godliness [maturity] has value [benefit] for all things, holding promise for both the present life and the life to come" (1 Tim. 4:8). Some of the promised benefits (blessings) that accompany godly maturity include an increasing capacity:

- to experience God and enjoy His presence (Heb. 12:14; Ezek. 44:10-16, 28; Ps. 27:4;   Phil. 3:7-11)

- to love others and experience their love in return (1 Cor. 13; Eph. 5)

- to discern the will, purposes, and wisdom of God (1 Cor. 2; James 1)

- to escape the corruption of the world and the schemes of the devil. (Rom. 12; Titus 3; 2 Cor. 2:11; Eph. 4:14-15)

- to be a good parent (Ps. 127; Eph. 4:14-15, 6:4)

- to enter into heaven with rewards and glory (2 Pet. 1:5-11; 1 Cor. 3:11-15; II Cor. 5:9-10)

- to stand without regret at the return of Christ (1 Cor. 3:11-15; 1 John 2:28-29)

- to participate in effective evangelism that glorifies God (John 17; Phil. 2:12-16; 1 Pet.3:15-16)

- to help others grow (Gal. 6:1-2)

- to endure trouble and take hold of the enabling grace of God

(Rom. 5:1-11; James 1:2-5)

- to understand and live through the power of the Cross (I Cor. 2:1-8; Phil. 2:1-16)

- to control one's speech and thus lessen relational conflict (James 3:13-4:3; Eph. 4:13-15, 29-32)

The true blessings of following Christ and growing to maturity are beyond our understanding (1 Cor. 2:9, Isa. 64:4). But receiving the blessings that accompany maturity requires hard choices. Jesus repeatedly urged His disciples, "Do not work for food that spoils, but for food that endures to eternal life, which the Son of Man will give you" (John 6: 27b). Scripture is filled with such admonitions, which encourage us to persevere (cf. Heb. 5:14; 2 Peter 1:10; 1 Cor. 3:10-15).

Justification by faith opens the gates of heaven and ushers believers into Paradise. But Scripture also affirms the rewards of faithfulness and obedience. Both of these enhance our citizenship in heaven. Unfortunately, many evangelicals don't receive thorough instruction about the conditions and prerequisites for many of heaven's blessings. Most of these conditional blessings have a direct link to mature obedience. (Rom. 2:6-10; 2 Pet. 1:10-11; Matt. 25:21; 2 Tim. 4:7-8).

Most of these conditional blessings have a direct link to mature obedience.

Maturity and Unity

Sometimes Christians need to separate from others in order to maintain purity of life and doctrine. But many of the divisions that plague Christians stem from immaturity. Mature believers are able to disagree about nonessential matters yet remain in unity. As Christians mature, they are better equipped to understand and appreciate those who hold different viewpoints. They allow room for God to reveal truth to others while humbly admitting that He might need to correct their own misconceptions. They're able to hold firmly to their convictions while remaining gracious and tolerant toward those who disagree. Often times mature believers must simply forebear (put up) with weakness and immaturity, bearing the burdens of others as they struggle to grow.

Many of the divisions that plague Christians stem from immaturity.

Mature believers also understand that some of the principles that govern the sanctification process are challenging to put into practice because they appear to conflict with other principles. Living a Christian life of balanced tension can only be achieved through "the wisdom that comes from heaven" (James 3:17). It's not an earthly wisdom, unspiritual and of the devil, but "first of all pure; then peace-loving, considerate, submissive, full of mercy and good fruit, impartial and sincere" (James 3:17).

According to James, God gives this wisdom to the single-minded, mature man, someone who's persevered through trials and is thus able to ask for and receive it from the hand of a Father who gives good and perfect gifts. On the other hand, immature people are like waves of the sea, blown and tossed by the wind, unstable in all they do. They can't understand or accept God's wisdom (James 1:2-8, 3:13-18). The Pharisees were examples of religious leaders who were unable to perceive who the Lord was or what He was doing.

Unstable, immature people often stress one biblical priority and neglect another. God makes it clear: we must strive to obey His Word no matter how much it challenges us. Living in the tension Scripture creates requires maturity. Mature believers can stay in step with God's Spirit as they trust in the Lord with all their hearts. They don't lean on their own limited understanding but acknowledge Him as the Sovereign Lord of a universe beyond what we know today (Prov. 3:5-6; Isa. 55:8).

Even a casual reading of Scripture underscores the truth that spiritual growth requires discipline and effort, self-denial and sacrifice.

Our infinite, all-knowing God has ways and means above the limits of a finite mind. He establishes truths that stretch our human understanding. Rather than throwing out one idea so we can accept another, we must live by faith, embracing what may seem like opposing principles. A few of the tension points that require mature wisdom include the following:

Balancing Divine Initiative and Human Responsibility

Even a casual reading of Scripture underscores the truth that spiritual growth requires discipline and effort, self-denial and sacrifice. Some confuse self-discipline with legalism, thinking anything in the Christian life that requires human effort couldn't come from God. We won't take time here to address this perspective (which stems more from Plato than Scripture), but we should remember the tension that exists. We have a responsibility to "work out [our] salvation with fear and trembling, for it is God who works in [us] to will and to act in order to fulfill his good purpose" (Phil. 2:13).

We must seek a balance between trusting the sovereign work of the Spirit to complete the work of sanctification and relying on human efforts and planning for spiritual growth. The Bible makes it clear that the Spirit aids and sustains our spiritual development. But it also shows that we have a responsibility (Phil. 2:12-13; Col. 1:28-29).

The Spirit of God is at work in us, but we are admonished to work ourselves, putting into practice what the Scripture commands (Philippians 2:12-13). As we obey the Word, our character and conduct are changed. Putting truth into practice calls for diligence and discipline. And this requires a plan.

Although God is the prime initiator and source of spiritual growth, Scripture reveals our need to follow the growth-governing patterns He has set up. In more than one place, Scripture compares the process to the work of a farmer, which includes seasons of planting, watering and fertilizing.

We can trust God with our work, and we can plan according to His desires (1 Cor. 3:6-8).

Balancing Positional and Experiential Truth

Some Scripture passages describe the work of God as complete or fulfilled. In other places, that same work is described as ongoing and incomplete, something that requires a daily putting into practice. Some examples include:

- We're set free from sin, but it has a grip on us that we must work to overcome (Rom. 6:6,12).

- We're saints, chosen ones, already made perfect in Christ with God Himself living and working in us. Yet we are also urged to "work out" this salvation we've received (Phil. 2:12), putting off the old self which is being corrupted and putting on the new self which is being transformed into His likeness

(Eph. 4:22-23).

- We're children of God, joint heirs with Christ, but we're in the process of being purified for a future in which we'll be fully like Him (1 John 3:2-3; Heb. 10:14).

Theologians sometimes refer to this dichotomy as the difference between *positional truth*, related to our current standing (or position) before God secured by Christ's death and resurrection, and *experiential truth*, truth we must put into practice in our everyday experience. As we mature, we learn to integrate these two aspects of our spiritual lives.

God through Christ accepts us fully and loves us unconditionally. We must teach this without compromise. But in order to live out that love and grace, we need both spiritual discipline and accountability.

In order to live out love and grace, we need both spiritual discipline and accountability.

A focus on positional truth without an emphasis on experiential truth can produce an inconsistent walk and an unfruitful life for Christ. A focus on experiential truth without a solid foundation of positional truth can lead either to legalism or to negativism and disappointment when hoped-for experiences don't arrive right away. Maturity helps maintain the balance and leads to continued growth.

Balancing the Now and the Not Yet

In some ways, the Kingdom of God has already come, and a fullness of grace accompanies it. We call this the *Now*. But parts of God's will don't find expression on earth until the King returns. And that's the *Not Yet*.

Some of the *Now/Not Yet* distinctives are clear. We know God is with us now in the person of His Holy Spirit although Christ has not yet returned to earth.

But sometimes we have more trouble knowing whether to wait for something God has said will occur (Not Yet) or to claim it by faith (Now). This explains the birth of the name it-claim it theology. Its supporters reason that since God's Kingdom has already come, our faith allows us to live in a "trouble-free zone" here on earth, naming our blessings and claiming them in Jesus' name. At first this appears logical, even biblical (as Phil. 4:13 says, "I can do all things through Him who strengthens me"). But the whole counsel of Scripture does not support it (cf. John 16:33b, "...in the world you have tribulation, but take courage: I have overcome the world").

In the familiar words of what has come to be known as the Lord's Prayer, Jesus urged His disciples to pray that God's Kingdom would come and His will would be done on earth as it is in heaven (Matt. 6:10). But which parts of God's Kingdom should we await in patience as not yet available? And which should we pray and work toward in faith as now available for those who tenaciously trust God?

When Christ appointed The Twelve (Luke 9:1-6; Mark 3:13-19; Matt. 10:1), He gave them tremendous authority. As He signaled the arrival of His Kingdom, He commissioned them to do three things: drive out evil spirits, heal the sick, and preach the good news of the Kingdom. Most believers agree that the good news is to be preached until the return of Christ. But confusion exists about how best to use Kingdom authority in ministries of healing and deliverance. These matters will no doubt produce questions till the Lord returns, but as believers mature, their discernment increases and they have better insight to sort out these and other tensions (Heb. 5:11-14).

Balancing Evangelism and Growth to Maturity

In terms of church history, the twentieth century was characterized by unprecedented evangelism and expansion. Hopefully, this trend will continue. Many hope to see a corresponding emphasis on growth to maturity characterize the twenty-first century and continue until Christ's return.

Scripture affirms that Christ will return to a bride who is holy and spotless, a church prepared for her husband. Certainly a people prepared and waiting for their King will experience revival and restoration. How do we get there from here? We get there through organizational models that move us toward renewal, and through prayer that seeks the outpouring of God's Spirit.

As we'll see in more detail later, Jesus said when a disciple is fully taught, he'll be like his teacher (Luke 6:40). This characterization links disciple building to the development of Christlike character and conduct. It's more than information-sharing or church programs, although both are important. But unless our disciple building strategies include the development of Christlike maturity, they fall short of the biblical model.

After washing His disciples' feet, Jesus stressed that as we follow His example and obey His commands to love one another, our prayers become powerful, our joy becomes full, our likeness to Him increases, and our witness is multiplied.

Our zeal for evangelism has increased, but our credibility as the people of God has decreased.

In recent generations, our zeal for evangelism has increased, but our credibility as the people of God has decreased. We've underemphasized the goal of becoming like Christ. As stewards of the gospel, we must reclaim this part of our spiritual heritage. We must, as Paul insisted, "present everyone fully mature in Christ" (Col. 1:28).

The Great Commission (Matt. 28:18-20) also emphasizes maturity. Here, Jesus stresses the imperative of world evangelization and church planting but includes the importance of obeying all of His teachings. Unless we are helping believers grow to the point where they are putting all of Christ's teachings into practice, we cannot claim to be fulfilling the Great Commission. We must take the gospel to the nations. But we must also train the nations to put all the truths of the gospel into practice. This requires much wisdom and effort. Christ promised to be with us, and we must do it.

Balancing Different Settings and Structures for Growth

Some people believe spiritual growth is best achieved and truth best applied through one-to-one relationships. For others, disciple building occurs best in a community setting, the ideal environment in which to "spur one another on toward love and good deeds" (Heb. 10:24). Others prefer corporate worship coupled with the robust preaching of God's Word in the public assembly as the best place for growth to occur. Some leaders cite the advantages of active involvement in ministry as a catalyst for growth (Philemon 6). Still others extol the value of study groups, and another group prefers the spiritual disciplines as the best approach to spiritual formation. So who has it right? Which method is best?

In truth, Jesus used all of these settings, and they all help promote growth. Our Lord trained His disciples within His larger ministry to the multitudes. The admonition to follow Him and become fishers of men (Matt. 4:19; Mark 1:17) would have meant little if Jesus hadn't been on His way to the crowds of Galilee. Our ministry refers to this dynamic as "building disciples in the midst of a movement." Although Jesus gave truth to crowds and cared about their welfare, He was careful to explain the applications to His small group in more private settings. On some occasions, He applied specific truth to one or two individuals.

The Scriptures speak of growth to maturity as a goal for both individuals and the entire Christian community.

The Scriptures speak of growth to maturity as a goal for both individuals and the entire Christian community (Col. 1:28-29; Eph. 4:11-13). To achieve this balance, church leaders must incorporate all dynamics and structures that encourage maturity into their approaches and programs.

Balancing Leadership Development and Equipping All Believers

Sometimes the maturing process in Scripture refers to preparing people for church leadership roles. Paul seemed to have this in mind when he admonished Timothy to entrust the "pattern of sound teaching" to faithful men who could transfer this truth to another generation of believers (2 Tim. 1:11-2:2). In other places, the Scriptures refer to church leaders as elders, spiritual shepherds, or overseers entrusted with the care and nurture of others (2 Pet. 5:1-3; Eph. 4:11-16). But growth to maturity is for every believer, not just the appointed leaders of the church. Our zeal to equip should extend to all believers (Col. 1:28-29).

In fact, growth to maturity should include both equipping leaders and assisting believers not yet ready for leadership roles. Leadership in the church differs from leadership in other settings. Of course, some important gifts and skills (charisma, initiative, communication, commanding presence, etc.) carry over into the church. God uses these abilities along with other gifts when He calls people into leadership. But the defining qualities for leaders in the church are character-driven, and godly character comes from equipping as a mature disciple (2 Tim. 3:1-13; Titus 1:5-9).

Regardless of their leadership ability, younger believers should not be appointed to leadership roles until they are spiritually mature enough for the challenge (1 Tim. 3:6, 10). On the other hand, mature Christians who may not possess natural leadership ability can function effectively in some leadership roles.

Part of Jesus' approach to help believers mature was the gradual development of leaders. At the right time, a leadership role can serve as a critical part of spiritual development. Growth occurs when believers trust and obey God and assume responsibility for others whether through an official church office or not. In fact, a leadership role may be as simple as the casual but definite task of a friend who works hard to encourage others.

A Proper Perspective

Three men digging a ditch on a scorching summer afternoon were approached by a passerby, who asked, "What are you guys doing?"

The first, already weary from exertion, responded impatiently, "What does it *look* like? We're digging a hole!"

The second added some information: "We're building a foundation pad. This hole's going to be filled with concrete."

The third man, who had been whistling happily while he labored, laid his shovel aside and wiped his forehead. He then explained how this particular hole would help them place one of the massive flying buttresses needed to support an entire wall of stained glass windows for a new cathedral. After describing in great detail the planned building process, he added, "See that rubbish pile? If things go according to plan, on Christmas Eve five years from now, my family and I will worship together at the altar in that same spot."

All three men were working hard at the same task. But their attitudes varied markedly with their perspectives. The man who could see the unseen had the best attitude and the most energy. Proper perspective enables us to survey a situation and see beyond what's happening to its significance and to develop strategies for what should happen next. Perspective provides hope when times are tough. And tough times are when hope emerges in mature people.

The root causes of our current crisis of maturity are complex, but as Christians, we must shoulder some of the responsibility. Though individual believers and some faith communities have found ways to grow and develop, the Church at large has lost much of the capacity to live in the world as salt and light. We haven't made growth toward spiritual maturity a primary goal the way Scripture commands (Matt. 28:18-20; Col. 1:27-29).

In essence, the maturation processes in the Church have either collapsed or been neglected. When maturation processes collapse, mature leaders fail to emerge. Without mature leaders, families suffer, churches neglect priorities, businesses fail, and in time, cultures crumble.

Without mature leaders, families suffer, churches neglect priorities, businesses fail, and in time, cultures crumble.

We're again at a pivot-point. Will this be our greatest catastrophe or our finest hour? It depends on our perspective of God and His Kingdom. Without a vision for maturity, it might be easy to lose hope and become weary. Are we digging ditches, or are we building something wonderful to the glory of God?

A Reason to Hope

There's growing evidence of an emerging movement that will

help us recapture a much-needed emphasis on maturity. Younger believers are searching for a more robust, biblical understanding of the gospel. A new generation of church leaders insists that the good news involves more than justification. It also includes growth to maturity. These leaders urge us to appreciate and apply the grace that forgives at every stage of the maturation process. This gospel-centered discipleship embraces a grace-driven process that encourages humility, produces relational honesty, and leads to maturity. Stressing the need for authentic community, spiritual growth, and good works, this process encourages believers to grow up.

John Burke sums up the need for an authentic maturity by saying:

> Our generation longs for something authentic. They are searching for "the real thing," though they don't really know what "the real thing" is. Because this generation has endured so much "me-ism" and letdown from those they were supposed to follow and trust, they want to see a genuine faith that works for less-than-perfect people before they are willing to trust. They want to know this God-thing is more than talk, talk, talk. They desperately want permission to be who they are with the hope of becoming more. They aren't willing to pretend, because hypocrisy repulses them. But most have yet to realize that every person is a hypocrite to some degree – the only question is whether we realize it and are honest about it. [16]

Jonathan Dodson says,

> The disciples of Jesus were always attached to other disciples. They lived in authentic community. They confessed their sins and struggles alongside their successes – questioning their Savior and casting out demons. They continually came back to Jesus as their Master and eventually as their Redeemer. As

the disciples grew in maturity, they did not grow beyond the need for their Redeemer. They returned to Him for forgiveness. As they began to multiply, the communities they formed did not graduate from the gospel that forgave and saved them. Instead, churches formed around their common need for Jesus. The gospel of Jesus became the unifying center of the church. As a result, the communities that formed preached Jesus, not only to those outside the church but also to one another inside the church. [17]

These men are right. The gospel Christ offers both justifies and sanctifies. May God strengthen their hands and increase their influence, and do the same for others like them. May He use them to drive back Satan and usher into the church a new season of Christlike maturity.

God is not unaware of or indifferent to the current crisis. In the past, He's sometimes hidden His prophets in caves, keeping them safe until a day of restoration dawns. He's sovereign over the nations (Psalm 2), Lord of His church, and ready to defend the honor of His name and renew His people. Throughout history, whenever it seemed as if the people of God were defeated, the troubles they faced became the catalyst for fresh hope, renewal, and victory.

Throughout history, whenever it seemed as if the people of God were defeated, the troubles they faced became the catalyst for fresh hope, renewal, and victory.

Sometimes refocusing perspective and building character requires hardship and defeat. Romans 8:28-29 affirms this as it reminds us, "God causes all things to work together for good to those who love Him, who have been called according to His purpose. For those God foreknew, He also predestined to be conformed to the likeness of His Son."

Helping people mature is not easy. Growing disciples face many obstacles, including the enemy, who hates the idea of mature believers. But satanic opposition, though real, is only one of the problems. As this chapter has shown, we seem to have lost our way or developed corporate amnesia regarding the process and priority of helping people mature. Lacking a clear strategy about how to help people grow, we opt for hit-or-miss tactics or repeat traditional approaches only because they're familiar.

The way *is* difficult and at times hard to understand. Discovering and implementing a process that produces maturity requires humility, courage, and faith. But the outcome is worth it, both now and for eternity.

Chapter 2

What is Maturity?

*God created us in His own image, and He desires
that we become like Him.*

What difference do you think it would make if all the
Christians in your community began behaving more
like Christ? What if, instead of squabbling over matters of style and personality, competing over programs and membership, or breaking fellowship over minor issues of doctrine, they
exhibited love as they deferred to one another?

What if more people trusted God to clarify matters as they patiently waited in prayer, even if it meant that they had to lose an argument or assume a less prominent position? What if honesty and
integrity marked every business transaction among believers? What
if political decisions were made for the public good and not to enhance the politicians' careers?

And what if evangelism extended beyond proselytizing to a genuine care of souls and doing of good works for the public good, and people became character-extensions of a good God who "sends rain on the righteous and the unrighteous" (Matt. 5:45)? What if those under authority had the faith to submit to God, trusting Him to work in and through the imperfect people He placed over them? What if those in authority, instead of "lording it over those entrusted to [their care]" (1 Pet. 5:3) listened to, and sometimes deferred to, those who followed them because they believed God could work through any member of His body? What if lay people were discerning enough to recognize and combat unbiblical worldviews corrupting the culture?

To say the least, such changes of conduct and character would be significant. Now multiply that impact for all the places Christians are located around the world, and you begin to understand God's agenda. *Maturity Matters.*

Three Developmental Periods

Maturation occurs throughout life. It begins the minute we're born, develops in our family of origin, progresses through our adult life, and is fully realized when we die and/or see Christ face to face. John the Apostle may have referred to this lifelong process in 1 John 2:12-14 when he mentioned "children," "fathers," and "young men." Three broad developmental periods of life contribute to our becoming and living as mature people:

1. The Formative Years at Home: This is the development that takes place in our family of origin from the time we're born until we fully enter adult life, leaving home and the family that raised us. What happens to us in childhood has a profound effect on future growth. This is the stage when our character, habits, and worldview take shape.

Childhood specialists disagree about the age when the transition to adulthood occurs. Thirteen seems to be a pivotal point in Scripture, with another milestone at age twenty. The scope of this book doesn't allow for a full discussion of this matter, but it seems likely that a season of transition begins at puberty and ends when a child leaves home. Regardless, we must recognize that the family of origin plays a significant part in the foundation and formation of maturity.

But Christians are not the only ones who can develop character and life skills in children. Unbelieving parents, because they still carry traces of God's image, can instill in their children honesty, integrity, industry, discipline, and other positive values. And, in a situation both ironic and tragic, Christian homes may espouse a biblical worldview and teach biblical doctrine but fail to provide an environment that fosters healthy relationships or nurtures secure emotional foundations.

2. Young Adulthood: After leaving home, young people must continue growing, becoming "mature and complete, not lacking anything" (James 1:4). When they reach this point of maturation, they don't cease to grow. Instead, they move forward, bringing all the tools and experiences they've been equipped with and press on to function as capable participants of an adult world.

In this period of time, the church must supplement and help complete the training begun in the home, teaching believers to "obey everything [Christ has] commanded" (Matt. 28:20). Many of those who followed Jesus while He was on earth were in this age group. For most people, this season of maturity should begin in adolescence and continue into the mid-to-late twenties or early thirties. For those who have experienced crippling loss, developmental problems, or a lack of childhood equipping, this stage may take longer or remain unfinished well into adult life. And some people fail to complete it altogether.

3. Mature Adulthood: This period begins after we're equipped as mature disciples and lasts until we die or meet Christ at His coming. It occurs after we've been trained to put all His commands into practice. In other words, this stage of development builds on the previous one. It doesn't mean we've fully arrived, no longer struggle, or need no further growth and application of truth.

But it does mean we have the capacity to finish well. We can age with grace and maturity because we've been trained to discern good from evil, learned to abide in Christ, and understand how to live well in a fallen world. It also means we have the skills and character to help others grow.

Achieving the goal of mature, godly character is complex and challenging.

Achieving the goal of mature, godly character is complex and challenging. We're complex beings made in God's image, and we face many hindrances to the process, including the enemy. In addition, believers often disagree about how growth occurs, what produces it, and what role church leaders should assume in facilitating it. Christian discipleship is a critical component in the maturity process. Although most evangelicals are committed in principle to building disciples, not everyone defines or applies the process in the same way.

A Point and a Process

As we learned in Chapter 1, Scripture indicates both that we can reach a point of maturity in our walk with Christ and also that we'll never reach maturity on this earth. The two statements are true at the same time, yielding another tension to maintain.

In one sense, we can reach a point of full training and equipping. We've learned to apply all the commands of Jesus and can process the struggles of this world with grace and perseverance. The Great Commission teaches this truth, and other passages support it (Matthew 28:20; James 1; Romans 5; Ephesians 4). But in another sense, we'll continue to mature, being progressively formed into the likeness of Christ as we endure hardship and press on to know the Lord (1 John 3:2-3; Phil. 3:12-14; 2 Cor. 3:18). In fact, God uses the trials of this world as a strategic part of the maturation process.

Persevering Through Trials

Several years ago, I hit a wall in my faith. Following Christ in ministry moved me into weariness and discouragement. Challenging confrontations with other Christian leaders had left me angry, jaded, and cynical. My own failures haunted me. In despair, I wondered if following Christ was worth the effort and began making plans to exit vocational ministry.

Out of my brokenness, I prayed. I asked God to make life easier so I could serve Him more efficiently, with greater focus and energy. A loving God answered my prayers with the birth of our fourth child, Elena Victoria. But her arrival didn't make life easier. Instead, our family faced significant challenges.

Elena's name means "the light that conquers the darkness," and from conception, she was destined to be different. My wife, Linda, had already experienced two miscarriages, and in her pregnancy with Elena, she struggled to avoid a third. Although Linda was bedridden for much of the time, Elena never made it to term. She arrived prematurely and entered the intensive-care neonatal unit.

But the difficult pregnancy and premature birth were only the beginning of Elena's trials (and ours). She required immediate surgery to survive her first day. Later, pulmonary procedures, more than a year of chemotherapy as she fought a rare form of leukemia, years of battling reactive airway disease, open-heart surgery, and multiple less serious incidents left her small body riddled with scars inside and out. (Did I mention Elena also has Down Syndrome?)

Scripture addresses a question on everyone's mind: Why does God allow suffering? The biblical answer is not unclear, just unpopular.

Why does God allow suffering? The biblical answer is not unclear, just unpopular.

The troubles and trials of this world serve a purpose: "For our light and momentary troubles are achieving for us an eternal glory that far outweighs them all" (2 Cor. 4:7). Peter says these troubles occur "so that the proven genuineness of your faith—of greater worth than gold, which perishes even though refined by fire—may result in praise, glory and honor when Jesus Christ is revealed" (1 Pet. 1:7). James urges that we should "Consider it pure joy, my brothers and sisters, whenever you face trials of many kinds, because you know that the testing of your faith produces perseverance. Let perseverance finish its work so that you *may be mature and complete*, not lacking anything" (James 1:2-4, emphasis added).

In the book of Romans, Paul states that the entire creation is groaning to be released into a new reality. This will occur on the day that we, the sons and daughters of God, are fully revealed with Christ (Rom. 8:22-23). Paul goes on to declare that God is sovereign over these trials. "We know that in all things God works for the good of those who love him ... to be conformed to the image of his Son" (Rom. 8:28-29a).

In still another place, Scripture affirms that God loves us deeply, as a parent loves a child. But parenting is *not* for the faint of heart; it often requires tough love. Like any good parent, God skillfully uses discipline. His correction involves training and instruction. "No discipline seems pleasant at the time, but painful. Later on, however, it produces a harvest of righteousness and peace *for those who have been trained by it*" (Heb. 12:11, emphasis added). This training process—

an essential part of life as Christ's disciple—helps us become the people we are in Christ, sons and daughters of a King who loves us.

Elena is now a young adult. God has used her to help me understand how much He loves me and how important I am to Him. I love her because she's my daughter. Like the rest of us, she's marred by The Fall, but her value stems from being created in the image of God. And she's defined by her Christlikeness.

Elena's capacity to forgive when wronged, to love unconditionally, and to celebrate life's simplest joys endear her to everyone. The joy she brings has nothing to do with her status or whether she can read, write, or communicate clearly. Yet in spite of this evidence in my own household, sometimes I still struggle with understanding and embracing my new identity in Christ. Too often, I forget I'm His much-loved child and He's accomplishing His plan in and through my life.

Too often, I forget I'm His much-loved child and He's accomplishing His plan in and through my life.

Who Are We?

And I'm not alone. Our culture—even our Christian culture—is desperate to understand who we are. Many items on our public agenda (human rights issues, abortion, cloning, stem cell research, evolution versus creative design, etc.) reflect the confusion that exists about our humanity.

And this is not only a contemporary dilemma. The psalmist framed the same question: "What is mankind that you are mindful of them?" (Psalm 8:4). Modern man still wonders, "Are humans just tissue that has evolved by chance and natural selection, or are we something nobler?"

Scripture affirms the truth: we are reflections of our Creator, beings with a purpose.

Scripture affirms the truth: we are reflections of our Creator, beings with a purpose. Christians hold to the conviction that we were created in the image of God to reflect His glory (Gen. 1:26-27). Other principles related to a biblical view of man include the following:

- **God's image in man is marred because of sin and the Fall.** This is more than a biblical observation. Countless wars, injustices, and inhumanities all reveal that something is wrong with the human race (Gen. 3:1-7).

- **Man is both dignified and depraved.** Though corrupted by sin, people still retain remnants of the divine image. In spite of our bent toward destroying the planet and each other, we retain the ability to produce great works of art, carry out tremendous feats of engineering, and demonstrate uncommon kindness and compassion (James 3:9).

- **Christ is the Second Man (Adam).** God became man and dwelt among us. Jesus came to seek and save that which was lost, and He has secured redemption and ultimate restoration for His followers (Rom. 8:29-30). He gives us His Spirit to enable us to keep His commandments and live godly lives as we wait for His reappearing (1 Cor. 15:45-49).

- **Christlikeness, or maturity, is God's goal for His people.** He wants us to reflect Him by being like Him as we wait for His return from heaven. He is thus glorified on earth among men and in heaven among the angels. This happens now through the church (Eph. 3).

Irenaus, one of the early church fathers, summed up God's intent by declaring, "The glory of God is man fully alive." [18] Jesus said, "The thief comes to steal, kill, and destroy. But I have come to give you life to the full!" (John 10:10; cf. Rom. 8:29-30).

- **Becoming Christlike requires following Christ.** Discipleship is a critical contributor to the maturation process. We follow Christ through a fallen world. Jesus said, "In this world you will have trouble. But take heart! I have overcome the world" (John 16:33). He also told His Father, "My prayer is not that you take them (My disciples) out of the world, but that you protect them from the evil one" (John 17:15). And of course, God has promised never to leave us or forsake us (Deut. 31:8; Heb. 13:5; Matt. 28:20b)

The process of being made fully alive in Christ, set apart and gradually changed for God's purposes and glory, is referred to by theologians, as sanctification.

The process of being made fully alive in Christ, set apart and gradually changed for God's purposes and glory, is referred to by theologians, as sanctification. This process includes, among other things, the mandate given to the Church to teach Christians to observe all that Christ commanded, thus being conformed to His likeness (Matt. 28:19-20).

Scripture also uses terms such as godliness, righteousness, or holiness to describe the idea of becoming Christlike. Of course, the fruit of the Holy Spirit also characterizes Christ Himself, for He was filled with "love, joy, peace, forbearance, kindness, goodness, faithfulness, gentleness and self-control" (Gal. 5:22-23).

As His mature followers consistently surrender to His Spirit, they exhibit these same Christlike characteristics. The theme of becoming mature, righteous members of God's Kingdom radiates throughout Scripture.

What Does Christlike Maturity Look Like?

But this raises the question: "What does it mean to manifest Christlike maturity? What does Christlikeness look like for us?" *The Nottingham Statement,* drafted by the Second Evangelical Anglican Congress in 1977, offers a summary definition of Christian maturity:

> Becoming mature in Christ involves both the deepening of our relationship with Him in repentance, faith and obedience, and the transforming into His likeness, which includes our thinking, behavior, attitudes, habits, and character. Together with growth in the knowledge of God and His truth, there should be a development in the capacity to distinguish between good and evil. The supreme glory of this maturing is the increasing ability to love and be loved in our relationship with God, the Church and the world. This transformation is accomplished by the action of the Holy Spirit, using the means of grace. [19]

Regarding Christlike maturity, Dr. J. I. Packer says,

> Genuine holiness is genuine Christlikeness, and genuine Christlikeness is genuine humanness—the only genuine humanness there is. Love in the service of God and others, humility and meekness under the divine hand, integrity of behavior expressing integration of character, wisdom with

faithfulness, boldness with prayerfulness, sorrow at people's sins, joy at the Father's goodness, and single-mindedness in seeking to please the Father morning, noon, and night, were qualities seen in Christ, the perfect man. Christians are meant to become human as Jesus was human. We are called to imitate these character qualities, with the help of the Holy Spirit, so that childish instability, inconsiderate self-seeking, pious play acting, and undiscerning pigheadedness that so frequently mar our professedly Christian lives are left behind. [20]

Christlike maturity has two interconnected aspects.

Christlike maturity has two interconnected aspects. One focuses on the devotional dimension and the other on the behavioral one. Maturity means, on the one hand, that we will increasingly love God Himself. Our devotion to Him will transform our hearts. This, in turn, will create a growing love for His Kingdom and His priorities. Our character and behavior will be transformed. John Piper affirms this by saying,

> Nothing fits a person to be more useful on earth than to be more ready for heaven. This is true because readiness for heaven means taking pleasure in beholding the Lord Jesus, and beholding the glory of the Lord means being changed into His likeness (2 Cor. 3:18). Nothing would bless this world more than more people who are more like Christ. For in likeness to Christ the world might see Christ. [21]

If we truly love God, we'll also love His people and His world. We'll serve Him not so much out of obligation or even gratitude but out of genuine love for who He is. He becomes the object of all our affections and longings so that everything else—even the good things He creates for us to enjoy—becomes secondary.

This theme repeats throughout Scripture. Jesus summarized it when He spelled out the requirements of the law in what has become known as the Great Commandment:

> One of the teachers of the law came and heard them debating. Noticing that Jesus had given them a good answer, he asked him, "Of all the commandments, which is the most important?"

> "The most important one," answered Jesus, "is this: 'Hear, O Israel: The Lord our God, the Lord is one. Love the Lord your God with all your heart and with all your soul and with all your mind and with all your strength.' The second is this: 'Love your neighbor as yourself.' There is no commandment greater than these" (Mark 12:30; cf. Deut. 6:5; Luke 10:27).

What it means to be Christlike: loving God supremely and loving others as we love ourselves.

These dual outcomes of love encompass what it means to be Christlike: loving God supremely and loving others as we love ourselves. And that describes Christ. He loves the Father and delights to do His bidding on earth and in heaven.

When it comes to biblical maturity, however, order is important. Devotion to God both precedes and produces Christlike morality and character. Jerry Bridges says it this way:

> Devotion to God is the mainspring of godly character. And this devotion is the only motivation for Christian behavior that is pleasing to God. This motivation is what separates the

godly person from the moral person, or the benevolent person, or the zealous person. It is sad that many Christians do not have this aura of godliness about them. They may be very talented and personable, or very busy in the Lord's work, or even apparently successful in some avenues of Christian service, and still not be godly. Why? Because they are not devoted to God. They may be devoted to a vision, or to a ministry, or to their own reputation as a Christian, but not to God. Godliness is more than Christian character: It is Christian character that springs from a devotion to God. But it is also true that devotion to God always results in godly character. [22]

I like to think of maturity as *thinking, feeling,* and *acting like Jesus.* In this sense, maturity means I'm able to see the world as Jesus sees it, I understand the principles that govern His Kingdom, and I have His compassion for those who hurt or struggle with sin. Maturity means I'm able to love and thus trust God deeply (but not perfectly). This love enables me to obey His commands as I follow the promptings of His Spirit. Maturity means when I'm wronged, I'm able to bless those who hurt me without retaliating, as Jesus did.

Maturity means I can generously and cheerfully give away my money, my energies, my time, and even my life if necessary.

Maturity means I can generously and cheerfully give away my money, my energies, my time, and even my life if necessary. I can sacrifice because I believe that in death there is glory and a resurrection to follow. Maturity matters (Titus 2:11-14; 2 Peter 3:16; 2 Corinthians

3:18).

Christlike maturity makes a profound difference on earth and glorifies God in heaven (Eph. 3:7-19). But is there a process that produces such maturity, helping people live and become like Christ? The answer is yes. And the process might surprise you because it's so familiar.

Most Christians are already familiar with the idea of discipleship, but this familiarity carries with it a danger.

Jesus said, "The student [disciple] is not above the teacher, but everyone who is fully trained will be like their teacher" (Luke 6:40). *Biblical discipleship is the foundation stone of Christlike maturity.* Most Christians are already familiar with the idea of discipleship, but this familiarity carries with it a danger. We must not allow familiarity with the term to diminish its significance or impact.

Much of what passes for discipleship in the modern church falls far short of what Jesus intended. Dallas Willard warned,

> My hope is to gain a fresh hearing for Jesus, especially among those who believe they already understand Him. In his case, quite frankly, presumed familiarity has led to unfamiliarity, unfamiliarity has led to contempt, and contempt has led to profound ignorance. [23]

Jesus spoke of discipleship as more than learning truths about God. He referred to it as a transformational experience, a process that changes people in a profound way to become like God, holy and righteous. People who consistently follow Christ know Him intimately, and He changes them forever. This is what Paul meant when he affirmed his ministry by saying, "We proclaim Him [Christ], admonishing every man and teaching every man with all wisdom, so that we may present every man complete in Christ. For this purpose also I labor, striving according to His power, which mightily works within me" (Col. 1:28-29, NASB).

A Needed Clarification

Sometimes when people hear the term *discipleship*, they think of rigid study programs or rigorous accountability. Others think of it as the follow-up (assimilation and teaching) that should occur after conversion. Some define it as "spiritual formation," which can mean anything from discovering spiritual gifts to mastering spiritual disciplines or embracing a mystical experience.

Still others insist there is no definitive process of spiritual development. They contend that because everyone is unique, it's impossible to develop programs that support spiritual growth. For them, discipleship involves total spontaneity and more often than not, unpredictability.

Unfortunately, some people have experienced spiritual abuse or manipulation under the false tutelage of so-called spiritual leaders. People like this tend to shun discipleship altogether. Because of the confusion regarding the term, let's redefine it. Here's a definition I like: "The intentional process, entrusted to the Church, where mature leaders help others progressively grow to Christlike maturity."

Discipleship is the intentional process, entrusted to the Church, where mature leaders help others progressively grow to Christlike maturity.

Paul urged Timothy to follow him as he followed Christ. This requires that we labor, "striving according to His power that mightily works within me" (Col. 1:29). Of course, this process is not easy. Busy church leaders often settle for traditions or methodologies that are simple to understand and apply but fail to achieve the key outcome of success: Christlike maturity.

We must resist the temptation to sacrifice a Christlike outcome for mere simplicity. A prominent American is reported to have said, "I wouldn't give a fig for the simplicity on *this* side of complexity; I would give my right arm for the simplicity on the *far* side of complexity." [24] Helping people arrive at true maturity may be complex, but we can understand, communicate and apply it simply.

After equipping His disciples, Jesus instructed these fully-taught followers to teach new disciples "to obey [put into practice] everything I have commanded you" (Matt. 28:20). As we'll see, His approach yielded maturity, and we can implement it in churches today. He taught relational, progressive truth as He exhorted His disciples to put His words into practice. He also challenged them to assume appropriate ministry responsibilities, praying that their faith would grow and their relationships with God and each other would deepen. He restored their hearts, helping them heal from past pain as He provided an environment where they could complete the developmental process begun in their family of origin. This growth didn't take place in a vacuum but in the midst of a community on mission.

The quality of bold, sacrificial love is the final outcome and evidence of a relationship with Him.

The quality of bold, sacrificial love is the final outcome and evidence of a relationship with Him (John 13:33-34.) Mature people are able to lay down their lives for a cause (or a Person) bigger than themselves: the Kingdom of heaven. Mature people glorify God and change the world.

One of this book's goals is to communicate an approach that helps church leaders devise strategies and implement programs for encouraging believers to grow to maturity in Christ. This approach involves more than understanding concepts. It also involves the development and deepening of faith: the ability to trust—in every situation of life—a good God who loves us. It requires sacrifice and devotion derived from a strongly-held conviction that the task is imperative.

Despite the urgency of the task, our relationship with God is also important. God is building something wonderful in and through His people. We serve Him as sons and daughters, not as His labor force. We work alongside our Father and in the process, come to know, understand, and love Him (Philippians 3).

Teaching Toward Maturity

God wants His people to progress to maturity and calls believers to grow up. One of our biggest needs today is a better understanding of the growth process and how to create growth environments. The modern Church must implement an effective way to develop mature lay leaders who have the ability to work alongside vocational church staff to equip the entire congregation. Paul refers to this process in his ministry and instruction to Timothy: "And the things you have heard me say in the presence of many witnesses entrust to reliable people who will also be qualified to teach others" (2 Tim. 2:2).

Paul, who had been training Timothy, now urged him to follow a "pattern of sound teaching" (2 Tim. 1:13) in training others. Paul's clear goal was to multiply himself and his ministry through Timothy and others like him. Moreover, Scripture instructs church leaders to have this same kind of ministry in the church as a whole.

So Christ himself gave the apostles, the prophets, the evangelists, the pastors and teachers, to equip his people for works of service, so that the body of Christ may be built up until we all reach unity in the faith and in the knowledge of the Son of God and become mature, attaining to the whole measure of the fullness of Christ (Eph. 4:11-13).

The biblical message is clear: Church leaders, using their gifts, must assume responsibility to disciple people in the congregation so they are equipped to minister to others. As the congregation develops, the whole church becomes involved in building itself up. This is necessary for the membership to reach unity and maturity and impact the world.

This maturation must involve a carefully-prepared training process: "You were taught, with regard to your former way of life, to put off the old self, which is being corrupted by its deceitful desires; to be made new in the attitude of your minds; and to put on the new self, *created to be like God in true righteousness and holiness*" (Eph. 4:22-24, emphasis added). This describes the sanctification process.

As we've already observed, the phraseology changes depending on the context, but the overarching process is repeated throughout the New Testament and always involves three components: You were taught, with regard to your former way of life, 1) to *put off your old self*, which is being corrupted by its deceitful desires; 2) to be made new in the attitude of your minds; and 3) to put on the new self, created to be like God in true righteousness and holiness.

The two actions of putting off our old self (1) and putting on our new self (3) are linked by another action: the renewal of our minds (2). Becoming Christlike involves receiving and applying truth about God and His Kingdom as well as truth about ourselves. Paul mentions this renewing of our minds as central to the transformational process when he states:

Therefore, I urge you, brothers and sisters, in view of God's mercy, to offer your bodies as a living sacrifice, holy and pleasing to God—this is your true and proper worship. Do not conform to the pattern of this world, *but be transformed by the renewing of your mind.* Then you will be able to test and approve what God's will is—his good, pleasing and perfect will (Rom. 12:1-2, emphasis added).

Where can we find a pattern that encourages the development of character and produces maturity?

But what is the pattern or process by which church leaders can train and instruct others in the congregation so that minds are renewed and people are able to put off the old self and put on the new? Where can we find a pattern that encourages the development of character and produces maturity? Must the modern Church use trial and error to figure it out? Should we only preach good sermons and trust that Christlike conduct will emerge? God will certainly use many means to equip us, but is there a more strategic method church leaders can employ?

The answer, of course, is yes. Jesus Himself gave us such a pattern to follow.

Chapter 3

Five Progressive Phases of Maturity

Maturity occurs gradually as we follow Christ through five progressive phases of spiritual development.

Jesus had a plan for bringing His disciples to maturity, and He transferred that plan to His Apostles to give to the churches. However, Christ's disciple building included more than evangelistic training and reproduction. It involved the development of character and followed a pattern that produced gradual growth so the follower would be "like his teacher" (John 6:40 NASB). Sacrificial love was the evidence of maturity as a disciple as well as the capstone of all His teaching: "By this everyone will know that you are My disciples, if you love one another" (John 13:35).

Peter echoed Christ's teaching, urging a progressive building of faith until the ultimate goal of *agape* (Christlike) love was attained (2 Pet. 1:5-9). Paul urged Timothy to reproduce the "pattern of sound teaching" in others and reminded him that the "goal of this instruction" was agape love (2 Tim. 1:13-14, 2:2). John taught that professions of faith without obedience and love are hypocritical (1 John 2:12-14, 2:3-6). Although progression to maturity is a hallmark of apostolic writing, it's difficult to discern the specifics of the pattern that guides the process from reading the Epistles alone.

The Gospels as a Guide

The description of the ministry of Jesus Christ given in the Gospels is the only place in Scripture where a progressive ministry model is fully developed. When we look at the Epistles, where admonitions to grow abound, we get a snapshot of what's happening in a particular situation at a particular point in time but with little or no sense of progression. The book of Acts shows progression in the spread of the Gospel but without enough detail to give us a specific pattern to observe and follow (although various sections of Scripture hint at such a pattern: Acts 20:27; 2 Tim. 1:13; Titus 1:5).

In the Gospels, we see Christ equipping His followers (The Twelve in particular) from their initial belief in Him to a point of maturity where He was able to leave a fledgling church in their hands. These Apostles believed that being involved with Christ throughout His earthly ministry was an important prerequisite for leadership in the Church (Acts 1:12-23).

Jesus prepared His disciples to have a ministry of their own under the power and guidance of the Holy Spirit.

Jesus prepared His disciples to have a ministry of their own under the power and guidance of the Holy Spirit. The Gospels show what He taught and the order in which He presented it. Luke 10 and the following chapters preserve what Jesus taught The Seventy, material nearly identical to His teachings for The Twelve. We see that Jesus taught truths in a particular order, designed for the progressive growth of each follower from first call until He left them. This pattern of sound teaching brought Jesus' disciples to a greater commitment and trust in Him. His training prepared them for ministry and, in the process, helped them grow to maturity.

A Panoramic Perspective

The Scriptures contain four Gospels, four different viewpoints of our Lord's life and ministry. By integrating them into one document, organized chronologically, biblical scholars provided a helpful tool for studying the life and ministry of Christ. This tool, called a Harmony of the Gospels, affords a progressive, panoramic perspective of the way Jesus conducted His ministry and trained His disciples.

At the conclusion of His ministry on earth, Jesus told His disciples to reproduce what He had done with them. This seems like a natural approach, because we all help others by relying on our own experience. But Jesus' final commission was not for His earthly disciples alone. It was given for our benefit, too, reminding us to look to the Gospels as a pattern for training. The repeatable, reproducible process revealed in Scripture produces maturity.

The repeatable, reproducible process revealed in Scripture produces maturity.

Dr. Robert Coleman is one of the pioneers of the modern discipleship movement. In his book *The Master Plan of Evangelism* (Revell, 1964; reprint ed. 2010), Coleman makes the observation that Jesus did everything with His disciples in mind. "His [Jesus'] concern was not with programs to reach the multitudes, but with men whom the multitudes would follow... Men were to be His method of winning the world to God." [25]

In one sense, the worldwide extension of Christ's Kingdom through the Church depended upon the equipping of those initial leaders. They were in the background of nearly everything Jesus said and did. WDA's Founder, Carl Wilson, expands this theme further in *With Christ in the School of Disciple Building* (NavPress, updated ed., 2009).

Beginning with the understanding that much of what Jesus did was for the benefit of Peter, James, John, and the other disciples changes how we view His ministry. We must look for trends, pivot-points, and strategic questions about what He did to equip them. Of course, His ministry extended beyond The Twelve, but what He did with His first disciples prepared them for leading the church.

A chronological study of the training ministry of our Lord using a Harmony of the Gospels as a guide reveals distinct phases in His disciple building approach. Each phase marks a major shift in how He equipped His leaders and helped them mature. Several questions emerge that help us better understand the process:

- What was the focus of His *teaching* in equipping His disciples?

- How did His *relationship* with the disciples develop and change?

- What did He *pray* for His followers?

- How did He *train* them for ministry?

- What *activities or situations* did He construct to serve as a catalyst for faith development?

- How did He meet their *emotional and relational needs*?

- How did He prepare them for *leadership*?

God understands this better than we do, and He patiently works with us to conform us to the image of His Son.

Growth does not occur overnight. Just as a newborn baby develops gradually, requiring much nourishment and proper care, so it is with the babe in Christ. A new Christian should expect to drink milk before he can eat meat and to crawl before he can walk. God understands this better than we do, and He patiently works with us to conform us to the image of His Son. We see this principle illustrated in the approach Christ took with His disciples as He helped them mature.

An Overview of the Equipping Ministry of Christ

At the outset of their ministries, both John the Baptist and Jesus called people to change their minds (repent) regarding their lives of sin and begin new lives through faith in God. They talked about the meaning of sin and warned of the coming judgment. They taught about God's love and His forgiveness of the sinner. Jesus was revealed as the Lamb of God who takes away the sins of the world. Many were converted and turned from their selfish, sinful lives to trust God and the promised Messiah.

Then Jesus called a group of disciples to spend intimate time with Him. He helped them understand His supernatural and heavenly origin, evidenced by His miracles. He taught them that He was the Messiah and showed them His deity and power as the glorious Son of God. As they developed a personal relationship with Him, they learned of His continued acceptance and forgiveness. They shared their new faith with others and learned to follow Him in obedience. They began to relate to each other as fellow believers.

As the disciples developed a personal relationship with Him, they learned of His continued acceptance and forgiveness.

Soon after this, Jesus called some of His disciples to be "fishers of men" (Matt. 4:19). They committed themselves to share in His public ministry, and He included them in His evangelistic campaigns. He taught them the principles of evangelism, showed them His love for sinners, and demonstrated His authority to forgive sin and give new life. He demonstrated His power over evil along with His authority to judge all men and to justify the believer at the resurrection. He taught His disciples about some of the differences between the two spiritual kingdoms, preparing them for the realities of spiritual warfare. He reinforced the importance of grace as the foundation of a relationship with God.

Eventually, after spending the entire night in prayer, Jesus chose The Twelve. He organized His ministry around this new group, instructing them and giving them authority. He portrayed and revealed Himself as God, the Lawgiver. His teaching focused on His new Kingdom: its blessings and the new law of inner righteousness. He contrasted the Kingdom of Heaven with Satan's kingdom and used parables to illustrate how God's Kingdom would grow.

Jesus showed His disciples that He was not offering merely a better life in this world, but eternal life—everlasting life of the highest quality. He precipitated a faith-crisis, causing them to reevaluate their expectations and trust God for the eternal things of life above the temporal. He challenged the status quo, revealing Himself again as the Lord from heaven. He taught divine authority over human authority and proclaimed assurance of eternal life and future glory.

Jesus precipitated a faith-crisis, causing them to reevaluate their expectations and trust God for the eternal things of life above the temporal.

As His fame and ministry grew and He prepared for His departure, Jesus appointed seventy other leaders to assist Him. He reinforced and enhanced earlier teaching for those who needed further application. The original Twelve assumed increased responsibility and ownership of the mission. They learned to trust their Master to work in other members of the community and to cope with outside opposition. He taught them about evils that would harm the Christian life.

The disciples discovered that mere human effort was inadequate for the Christian life.

Unfortunately, as The Twelve assumed new responsibilities, they relied more on themselves than on God. But through their failures along with the realities of the crucifixion and resurrection, they discovered that mere human effort was inadequate for the Christian life. They learned of God's sovereignty and the all-sufficiency of Christ in and through His Holy Spirit. They learned that His Kingdom was not confined to Israel but extended worldwide. A paradigm for the

Church emerged and before long, Christ commissioned them to make disciples of all nations. He exhorted them to transfer the training they had received to others, urging these new disciples to follow Him in obedience and become like Him.

Jesus' approach reveals both progression and intentionality. He was preparing leaders for maturity, training them in such a way that after His departure, they could reproduce what they had seen and learned. Then, in sending His Spirit, He reminded them of His equipping principles and process. He also led them into a deeper understanding of how to apply this in the Church (John 14:26).

Although the Spirit amplified their training and provided the power to follow Him, rather than attempting to replace the pattern of sound teaching Jesus employed, the disciples built upon it. The progressive growth effected through the ministry of God the Spirit is similar to the phases of spiritual development evidenced in the ministry of God the Son. Working in concert with the Spirit, church leaders can follow the same progressive process to equip modern disciples that Jesus used to train and deploy the first church leaders.

What Jesus Did – What We Can Do

A closer look at the Gospels reveals five distinct phases of spiritual development Jesus used to equip His disciples. Modern believers progress through similar stages until we also become mature. In this sense, becoming mature doesn't mean we stop growing or have ceased needing to grow. It means that, like the first disciples, we've been equipped to put all the teachings of Christ into practice (Matt. 28:20; cf. Col. 1:28; Eph. 4). From this point, we have the capacity to continue maturing, being transformed from glory to glory into His likeness (2 Cor. 3:18). By studying the phases of spiritual growth in Christ's ministry, we can gain insight into how the Holy Spirit will help us grow and how church leaders can participate in this equipping process.

Phase I: Establishing Faith

The initial step of faith in becoming a disciple of Christ is to repent and believe. This involves leaving our old way of life and trusting in Christ as Savior and Lord. This event is referred to in Scripture as being "born again" (John 3). Whether a person comes to faith at age eight or age eighty-eight, he becomes a newborn babe in Christ the moment he repents and believes.

Jesus' ministry actually began with that of John the Baptist. It was John's call to prepare the way for the Messiah (John 1:23) and to identify Him to God's chosen people, the Jews (John 1:29). John prepared the way for Jesus by preaching the Gospel (Luke 3:18) and calling people to come to the Messiah through repentance and faith. He exhorted them to be baptized as a sign of their repentance. We know John's ministry was effective because of the witness of Scripture that people went out to hear Him "from Jerusalem and all Judea and the whole region of the Jordan" (Matt. 3:5).

As John's ministry progressed, he gathered a group of disciples according to the custom of the day. John's disciples were people who received his message, were baptized by him, and identified with his movement. They spent time with John on a regular basis and had an opportunity to hear his message on many occasions.

John's message contained various components of the Gospel message, including the following themes or emphases: repentance and its fruits, faith in the Messiah's coming, baptism, the Holy Spirit, and judgment.

These components communicated the Gospel message of repentance and faith. As John repeated these themes, he reinforced the concepts in his first disciples. Interestingly, the book of Hebrews lists six "elementary teachings" that must be understood as part of an initial foundation before believers can move ahead to maturity in Christ.

Therefore let us move beyond the elementary teachings about Christ and be taken forward to maturity, not laying again the foundation of repentance from acts that lead to death, and of faith in God, instruction about cleansing rites, the laying on of hands, the resurrection of the dead, and eternal judgment (Heb. 6:1-2).

There is an amazing correspondence between the themes John emphasized and the elementary teachings described here. The "laying on of hands" is probably a reference to the practice in the early church of laying on hands at baptism to symbolize that those being baptized had received the Holy Spirit.

Many modern believers have never had anyone help ground them in these foundational doctrines and first steps of faith.

All new believers need an opportunity to gain and review a more complete understanding of the components of the Gospel. This serves as a starting point for their Christian growth. Sadly, many modern believers have never had anyone help ground them in these foundational doctrines and first steps of faith. Because of this, they often struggle with doubts and confusion regarding their Christian conversion experience.

John's ministry of repentance provided the initial evangelistic thrust that helped launch Christ's ministry. (Jesus' first disciples, in fact, initially followed John.) John preached for about six months before Christ started His ministry. At that point, John continued his work as a parallel ministry of evangelism until his arrest and execution. Afterward, some of John's scattered disciples continued to look for "the one coming after" John until they came to understand that Jesus was the promised Messiah (Acts 19:1-7).

Phase II: Laying Foundations

This next phase in the believer's life focuses on gaining a better understanding of who Christ is and how to follow Him. As the new Christian learns more of Christ's nature and character, he learns to trust Him not only for eternal salvation but for subsequent matters as well.

During this phase, Jesus invited His disciples to spend more time with Him so He could reveal Himself more fully. He invited a few of John's disciples to be His followers, too. John had singled Christ out to his disciples as the "Lamb of God" (John 1:35-41).

As Jesus gathered more followers, these first disciples recruited others. In this way, He quickly pulled together a group of His own disciples. But during this phase, His ministry didn't become large. Noting this, some theologians refer to this phase of ministry as the "year of obscurity." [26] This phase, in which Jesus led a small community, lasted only about six to nine months. However, the lack of public visibility does not imply a lack of significance.

Jesus' primary emphasis during this period was to reveal Himself to His followers and build a relationship with them.

Jesus' primary emphasis during this period was to reveal Himself to His followers and build a relationship with them. So He kept His ministry small and spent a great deal of time with His disciples, forging relationships and building trust. During this period, these early disciples became convinced that they had found the Messiah (John 1:35-51). They had not yet left their vocational jobs to travel with Him full-time, but He did take them on a couple of journeys, building friendships as He modeled ministry.

Few people have a comprehensive view of God when they first trust Him. They come to Him—often in desperation—hoping He will make a difference in their lives. One of the first things young believers need is a more comprehensive picture of who Jesus Christ is and how much He loves and accepts them. This is exactly what Jesus did for His first followers. He revealed Himself by making claims as The Messiah and confirmed them through two significant miracles: turning water into wine and raising the son of a royal official from the dead (John 2, 4).

New Christians today need the same things as the first disciples.

New Christians today need the same things as the first disciples. They need to gather in a small community of other believers and learn about who Jesus is, how to build a relationship with Him, and how to begin to trust and follow Him. These community groups become focal points of a new spiritual family, a place where many relational and emotional needs are met. They need to see God answer their prayers and begin to meet their needs. They need a leader who will model the Christian life before them and build a relationship with them.

During this phase of ministry, Jesus modeled many aspects of the Christian life. He modeled spending time with the Father and walking in dependence on Him. He also modeled what He would ask His followers to do next. Jesus kept this pattern throughout His ministry, never challenging His disciples to do anything they had not first seen Him do. Especially during the foundational season, modern believers also need to see leaders modeling the Christian life and ministry.

These examples set the tone and environment for much of the growth to come.

Anticipating a period of evangelism training, Jesus also modeled outreach during this season, offering grace and salvation to those in need. He reached out to the religious leaders when He told Nicodemus, "You must be born again" (John 3:7). He reached out to the downtrodden when He offered living water to the woman at the well (John 4:1-26). And He offered acceptance to those who felt ostracized by the religious establishment. As a result, many came to Christ in the Judean countryside where He retreated to spend time with His disciples (John 3:22).

Today's new believers will feel comfortable inviting their non-Christian family members, colleagues, and friends to participate in their new community of faith if they feel sure grace and acceptance are present there. As these outsiders experience the love and acceptance of Christ evidenced through His church, many will also become Christians.

In our zeal for more outreach and church growth, we often neglect the development of new believers.

Unfortunately, in our zeal for more outreach and church growth (both commendable outcomes), modern evangelicals often neglect the development of new believers. Instead of giving them time to internalize the truths about God, themselves, and how to live the Christian life, we rush them into active ministry service. As a result, their growth is stunted, and they can't form the spiritual foundations that will enable them to stand firm when trials come.

In addition, a lack of emphasis on true discipleship implies that ministry is more important than personal development and spiritual growth. This is an unnecessary tragedy. If modern leaders understood the foolish consequences of putting young believers into leadership roles too soon, they would never do it. But, as we've seen, modern traditions often overrule biblical principles and wisdom.

I appeal to today's church leaders to provide all new believers (and many older believers who lack a solid spiritual base) with the opportunity to establish this critical foundation for ongoing faith development. To address what we believe is a deficit in spiritual development, WDA offers Cornerstone, a year-long learning experience for a community group or a mentor relationship. But there are many other excellent resources for laying foundations.[27]

The mentor must be a good role model.

At this time in a disciple's life, a faithful mentor (life coach) is an important key to growth. Since we learn much of our faith from the examples of others, the mentor must be a good role model. He must spend time with Christ, share Christ with others, trust Christ to meet his needs, and exhibit enthusiasm and a commitment to spiritual growth.

At this phase, Jesus strategically involved his young disciples in the ministry, giving them important and necessary tasks. They told others about their experience of finding the Messiah, and Jesus had them baptize people who began to follow Him. (In His day, baptism was not something performed primarily by ordained clergy.) Jesus had His disciples purchase and distribute food, manage money, provide transportation, and more. This helped assimilate them into His movement and understand the importance of their part in His Kingdom. But the tasks He assigned did not include leadership roles or anything that could either lead to spiritual embarrassment or challenge their faith beyond its depth.

As new believers start developing a relationship with Christ, they see answers to prayer and experience changed lives. Next, they become more excited about their new life of following Christ. At this time, many of them will begin to tell others about Christ, a natural outcome of their experience that mentors should encourage. Often, new Christians begin to want more of their mentor's time along with information that will help them grow. As we observe these developments, we should realize their growing readiness for the next phase of disciple building: Equipping for Ministry.

Phase III: Equipping for Ministry

In this phase, a disciple learns to serve others and engage in ministry opportunities under the guidance of more mature believers. In the Gospels, this occurred as Jesus challenged some of His disciples to "Follow Me, and I will make you fishers of men" (Matt. 4:19 NASB). This call indicated that He was moving them to the next phase of growth. Once they decided to accept this invitation to minister alongside Him, Jesus took His disciples along on a mission trip, where He taught and ministered to others and gave The Twelve increased responsibility and opportunity to communicate the Good News.

Jesus launched this period of ministry by making two major changes. The first was a shift from private to public ministry. Up until this point, He had served primarily in remote areas. But this new season marked a shift to the public arena. He accomplished this by healing many people and casting out demons, which tended to attract attention (Luke 4:31-44). Crowds began following Him, and the movement quickly expanded. As interest grew, Jesus began His public teaching ministry, which continued until the end of His time on earth.

The second change in Jesus' ministry involved His challenge to make His disciples "fishers of men" (Matt. 4:19, NASB). This seemed to include most of His early followers. He later added Matthew and possibly others as well. Scripture does not make clear how many people He challenged in this way, but by the end of this phase, the group probably included all of those He would later appoint as Apostles, and possibly some of The Seventy as well.

Jesus then took His disciples on a series of evangelistic tours. His method of training at this point was fairly simple: He included the disciples in His evangelistic outreach. Because of the public miracles, He attracted a large, interested crowd wherever He went. But not everyone could get close to Jesus in person. This growing public ministry created many private opportunities for His disciples to share their faith and experience, explaining who Jesus was and what He had done for them.

We should teach our disciples how to present the Gospel.

In the same way, we need to challenge those who are ready to join a ministry-training group. We should teach our disciples how to present the Gospel, communicate the Good News by using their testimonies, and relate to non-believers. We should provide opportunities for them to share the Gospel with those interested in knowing more about Jesus. As they see people respond to their message, their faith will deepen.

During this period, Jesus' method of teaching involved placing His disciples in situations that forced them to sort out issues related to legalism and the freedom they enjoyed in their relationship to Him. He did this by creating Sabbath controversies. Healing someone on the Sabbath, for example, created a debate about the Sabbath laws. This provided a forum to teach about His identity as Lord and, at the same time, expose the legalism and inadequacy of the Jewish leadership. It also created an opportunity for Him to teach healthy perspectives on ministry and freedom in the Christian walk.

The teaching in this phase came as an outgrowth of Christ's evangelistic ministry. Through repeated presentations of the Gospel, Jesus' disciples heard more and more about its benefits. In addition, they encountered difficulties and opposition that gave them more opportunities to learn.

As our own disciples become involved in sharing the Gospel, they too will grow in their appreciation of what Christ has done for them, and they too will run into problems as they meet people with differing beliefs. This will create opportunities to clarify truth and help them continue to grow.

Jesus modeled mature leadership by showing compassion for hurting people; making the most of the natural opportunities for ministry that came His way every day; teaching with authority; proclaiming the Gospel boldly; continuing to reach out to new people; and demonstrating His power over demons, sickness, and disease. He involved His disciples in many of these activities during this Phase III experience and modeled others in anticipation of Phase IV.

Phase III is an important period for helping people understand their new identity as believers. As The Twelve served alongside Jesus as "fishers of men," they better understood their new role and position in the Kingdom. The instruction Jesus gave regarding law and grace also clarifies the believer's identity in Christ (the same approach taken by Paul in the Epistles).

A new relationship with God begins when someone believes in Christ as Lord and Savior, trusting His substitutionary death for sin that reconciles us to God. Scripture affirms that when this occurs someone is "born again" through His Spirit and receives a new identity as a "child of God" (John 3:3-8; Rom. 8:12-16; 2 Cor. 5:17-18a). But in addition to being accepted in Christ, believers are also invited to participate with God in building and extending His Kingdom (2 Cor. 5:18b-20). This "ministry of reconciliation" serves to further clarify our new identity in Christ as royal children who serve as royal ambassadors.

This "ministry of reconciliation" serves to further clarify our new identity in Christ as royal children who serve as royal ambassadors.

In one sense, God doesn't need us to accomplish His plans and purposes. He is, after all, Almighty God. But He calls and invites us to minister alongside Him, linking the success of His mission on earth to our active participation (Rom. 10:14-15).

Sharing the Gospel is a catalyst for further understanding (Philemon 6). Realizing that God's plan for extending His Kingdom includes this strategic role for us provides great hope and encouragement. We, who once were enemies of God, are now His children, allies, and partners. We are citizens and servants of heaven, ambassadors of an eternal King!

We, who once were enemies of God, are now His children, allies, and partners.

In Phases II and III, we lay the foundation for Christian growth and equip people for ministry. But not everyone challenged for ministry training progresses to immediate leadership. Some require more time to grow and experience the restoration that accompanies walking with Christ. And sometimes, God's call to leadership is a matter of timing and opportunity. We should encourage disciples to aspire to leadership but not rush to appoint people to premature positions. Scripture warns of harmful and unintended consequences of laying hands on people too quickly (1 Tim. 3:6-5:22). As if to underscore the importance of Phase IV, the Lord prayed all night before appointing The Twelve. In the same way, we need to wait for the Spirit to confirm His calling, gifting, and timing. Phase III serves as an excellent filter for recognizing and selecting future leaders. It also helps determine the appropriate pace and degree of involvement.

Phase IV: Developing New Leaders

When a believer progresses to this phase, he is ready to take responsibility for the spiritual development and well-being of others. During this period, Jesus taught His disciples how to live in His Kingdom. In addition, He appointed The Twelve to be Apostles*, sending them out on their own to preach the Kingdom of God and to minister

---

*The term Apostle (literally: "sent one") has a unique meaning and usage when it refers to the commissioning of The Twelve and others (such as Paul, Barnabas, et al) who were the formative, foundational establishers of The Church (2 Cor. 12:11-12). This type of Apostleship, or proximity to an Apostle as in the case of Luke, was one of the markers for the acceptance of their writing into the Scriptural canon.

The gift of apostleship (1 Cor. 12:28 and Ephesians 4) seems to refer to those who had the gift of being a church planter, though not in the same sense as the original Apostles, and as such applies throughout the Church age.

Not every church leader (overseer/elder) has the gift of apostleship. But all leaders need to be equipped and authority conveyed to them through the laying on of hands. This is the affirmation of the church that these leaders have been trained and examined in matters of doctrine, character, mission, etc. and thus retain spiritual authority to carry out their calling.

to people's needs. Mark 3:14-15 summarizes what Jesus did during this phase: "He appointed twelve, designating them apostles, that they might be with Him and that He might send them out to preach and to have authority to cast out demons."

This phase actually had two parts. The first involved appointing and instructing His new leaders in Kingdom principles. The second involved Christ creating a series of situations that forced His leaders to reevaluate their expectations of what it meant to follow Him. Both then and now, this reevaluation crisis is pivotal. It centers on leaders choosing either the eternal benefits of following Christ or leadership roles that grant them temporal power and success.

As Jesus began this new phase in His ministry, He prayed all night (Luke 6:12). This unusual occurrence signaled that something important was about to happen. Jesus called all His disciples together and appointed The Twelve as Apostles, the core of His leadership team. It's clear that He was preparing them for their future ministry assignment, when He would send them into all the world (*apostle* actually means "sent one," or missionary.) [28]

Jesus' appointment of The Twelve marked the beginning of a two-year training process designed to prepare them for the day He would leave them in charge of the Church. But rather than send them out at this point to start their own ministry, He drew them closer and spent more time teaching and being with them.

Throughout His ministry, Jesus gradually required more and more from His disciples in both time and commitment.

This marks an important element for modern disciple builders. Throughout His ministry, Jesus gradually required more and more from His disciples in both time and commitment. In turn, He also gave them more of His time and focused attention.

Our tendency in the modern church is to give developing leaders more responsibility but not more time. We would be wise to follow Christ's example and spend significant amounts of time building relationships with and developing these new leaders.

Also in Phase IV, Jesus sent His new leaders out to preach and gave them authority to heal and cast out demons (Luke 9:1-9). Jesus began doing these activities Himself during Phase III. Having modeled them, He now gave The Twelve the same responsibilities and authority in Phase IV. As we've already observed, Jesus modeled the activities He would assign to His disciples before He asked them to perform as He did.

The word translated, *preach* has a wide range of meanings: from preaching the Gospel to teaching doctrines. In this setting it seems to indicate that The Twelve now had the responsibility and privilege to expand Jesus' preaching and teaching. For the first time, they shared His preaching duties, proclaiming His Kingdom and exercising His authority. More than likely, they helped the new followers (those who had come to faith during the outreaches of Phase III) establish the same foundation they had received. Communicating these truths reinforced them in the hearts of The Twelve. At this point, Jesus' delegation of responsibility and authority was profound. The Apostles would each continue this practice until they died.

For the first time, they shared His preaching duties, proclaiming His Kingdom and exercising His authority.

Now that the Canon of Scripture is complete, contemporary "sent ones" don't have the same authority and responsibility as The Twelve for revealing new truths about God and His Kingdom. But there remains real authority to announce His Kingdom and extend it into all the earth. This authority includes the power to triumph over demons and unclean spirits, "binding the strong man" so a unified church can, in effect, "spoil the goods" of Satan, rescuing people from the dominion of darkness and enabling them (through the Gospel) to be transferred to the Kingdom of the Beloved Son (cf. Matt. 12:25-29; Col. 1:13).

In this phase, Jesus gave His leaders the authority to cast out demons and heal the sick. Before sending them out (cf. Luke 9:1-2; Mark 3:14-15), He gave a great deal of instruction and some additional modeling about how to conduct spiritual warfare. By teaching the parables of the Kingdom, He also gave them more instruction on the type of warfare they would face.

Spiritual warfare in the modern church is often characterized by extremes. It seems we either focus too much or not enough attention on the evil one and his schemes. Jesus provided a balanced approach, giving His disciples progressive training in this area. The disciple building instruction and experiences of Phases II through the first half of Phase IV parallel and represent what Paul referred to as "put[ting] on the full armor of God" (Eph. 6:10-18).

In Phase II, Jesus' disciples learned they could be confident that Christ was their Savior and King: the equivalent of putting on the "helmet of salvation" (Eph. 6:17). In Phase III, Jesus modeled spiritual warfare by casting demons out of many people and healing others, thus demonstrating His authority over all His creation, including Satan and his demonic forces. He also trained His disciples in evangelism, in essence fitting their feet "with the readiness that comes from the gospel of peace" (Eph. 6:15). Also in Phase III, much of Jesus' teaching focused on His disciples' position in Christ. This concept relates directly to putting on the "breastplate of righteousness" (Eph.

6:14).

Throughout the first three phases and into Phase IV, Jesus taught His disciples a variety of foundational truths needed to resist and defeat the devil. He understood the challenges of the Christian life. The evil one's weapons of choice are lies: wayward thoughts, suggestions, subtle accusations, etc. The battles are fought close at hand, occurring in areas where our past pain makes us most vulnerable and affecting our deepest relationships.

Jesus understood the challenges of the Christian life.

This hand-to-hand combat requires both the "sword of the Spirit" (Eph. 6:17) and the "shield of faith" (Eph. 6:16). The truths of the Word give us the ability to rebuke the evil one for his lies while simultaneously enabling us to persevere, resisting the "roaring lion" (1 Pet. 5:8), trusting God, and eventually seeing the evil one flee as, in the process, we mature (1 Pet. 5:8-10).

Once the disciples had completed their spiritual warfare training, Jesus sent them out with authority to cast out demons. He also modeled how to pray for protection from the evil one (John 17; Eph. 6:18-20). We need all of these weapons to protect us against Satan's counterattacks as we move into his territory and take back what he has controlled. Jesus knew this. He gave The Twelve the weapons they needed, and He does the same for us.

He gave The Twelve the weapons they needed, and He does the same for us.

As already stated, during this period Jesus spent a lot of time teaching His disciples. In the first part of Phase IV, He taught primarily about the Kingdom of God in two major sections of Scripture: the Sermon on the Mount and the parables of the Kingdom. The Sermon on the Mount is considered Christ's most important and central set of instructions, the highlight of everything He taught. This Sermon set forth the standards for those who would be a part of the Kingdom of God and who would lead. It unveiled Christ as the Old Testament Law-giver (God Himself) and clarified how the Law integrates with His New Covenant through His Spirit (a work of grace which occurs first in the heart and gradually works outward to affect all of life). In addition, His teaching in the Sermon helped prepare His disciples (all Jews) for their role as leaders of the Church among the Gentile nations.

His teaching in the Sermon helped prepare His disciples (all Jews) for their role as leaders of the Church among the Gentile nations.

It is important to understand that Jesus did not introduce the concept of law (standards of righteousness) to His disciples until after He had been with them for some time. This stood in marked contrast to the Pharisees, who built their entire ministry on the Law. Instead, in Phase II, Jesus first built a solid relationship of unconditional love. In Phase III, He emphasized grace as the ongoing basis of His relationship with them. It is not until Phase IV that He introduced the concept of law.

When we understand that Christianity is primarily a relationship with Christ, not a set of rules, and that this relationship is based on grace rather than a set of rules, we're able to consider how we can best please God. At this point in the maturation process, we begin to see the benefits of being conformed to the likeness of Christ our King.

As King and Law-Giver, He wants us to live according to His Kingdom principles, most of which are revealed in The Sermon on the Mount. These principles of righteous living (law) then become a way for us to please God, because we love Him and are motivated by this love (2 Cor. 5:14). Rather than throwing out the law, the mature Christian sees its proper place. Law gives wisdom and guidance to those who want to please God, a fitting response to the love and grace He has shown them.

About halfway through this Phase, Jesus sent The Twelve out in pairs to do evangelism. This time, they used a different manner of outreach than in Phase III. He sent them into villages ahead of Him with specific instructions: take no money and stay only in places where the Gospel was welcomed. This approach required plenty of faith and courage, qualities of those who had progressed in maturity. Modern evangelism trainers could benefit from Jesus' example of progressive evangelism instruction.

In Phase II, there was an excited anticipation of the revealed Messiah accompanied by forgiveness, grace, and unconditional acceptance when new disciples were welcomed. In Phase III, the initial miracles of Jesus and His teaching created interest and curiosity, a non-threatening environment where His disciples could entertain questions about Him from the crowd of onlookers and share their personal experiences. After they became accustomed to sharing their faith this way, Jesus prepared them for more difficult situations.

In Phase IV, He sent them out in pairs without accompanying them. Later, He took them into Gentile regions, thus exposing them to cross-cultural evangelistic opportunities. Jesus gradually moved from less-threatening types of evangelism to more difficult and diverse types. At the end of His ministry, Jesus commissioned His disciples to take the Gospel to the whole (Gentile) world where they repeatedly encountered hostility and opposition. At the close of their training, they were mature enough to handle this challenge.

In the second half of Phase IV, something traumatic and pivotal occurred.

In the second half of Phase IV, something traumatic and pivotal occurred. Jesus placed His leaders in situations that forced them to reevaluate their expectations and understanding of His Kingdom and rule. Up until this point, the ministry had been generally well-accepted by the crowds, with little resistance and growing popularity. Association with Jesus was considered beneficial. But all this was about to change.

Right at this time, Jesus took steps to purge His ministry. John 6 tells us that after He fed the multitudes, the crowd wanted to escort Him to Jerusalem and make Him king. But He never intended to be the king they wanted, a ruler who would meet their earthly expectations and satisfy their selfish demands.

Instead of accepting a temporal coronation, He preached a very difficult sermon that rejected their offer and exposed their wrong motives.

Instead of accepting a temporal coronation, He preached a very difficult sermon that rejected their offer and exposed their wrong motives (John 6:25-59). As a result, many of His so-called disciples, those who followed Him from selfish motives, stopped walking with Him (John 6:60-66). This may have been the point when Judas began to scheme and plot against Him. Even Peter and the other Apostles were confused, but they recognized the eternal significance of the unfolding events (John 6:67-69). In addition, Jesus' refusal of an earthly kingdom in favor of an eternal reign coupled with his rebuke of those who followed Him for temporal gain increased opposition to His ministry and moved those who remained to reevaluate their priorities. We must understand that, rather than avoid a clash of values and worldviews, Jesus chose to initiate this crisis. Modern disciples and disciple builders should expect nothing less. The Spirit will create situations that cause us to want to stop following Christ.

Instead of quitting, we need to reevaluate our priorities, put our hope in eternal things, and encourage one another to persevere (James 1). As we persevere, God changes our perspective, makes us more like Christ, gives us new reason to hope, and reveals His deep love (Rom. 5:1-5). This is how maturity occurs and what its fruit looks like. Like everything Jesus prepares and orchestrates, the process isn't easy, simple, or painless, but truly beneficial.

As a result of being discipled in this way, Peter could say with conviction that we should "not be surprised at the fiery ordeal that has come on you to test you, as though something strange were happening to you. But rejoice inasmuch as you participate in the sufferings of Christ, so that you may be overjoyed when his glory is revealed" (1 Pet. 4:12-13). Earlier, he said that these trials occur "so that the proven genuineness of your faith—of greater worth than gold, which perishes even though refined by fire—may result in praise, glory and honor when Jesus Christ is revealed" (1 Pet. 1:7).

But if we understand God's character and nature, our ability to persevere during tribulation increases. We must again underscore the importance of helping new believers build their spiritual foundations during Phases I and II. This aids the development of maturity during the fourth phase. Because Peter had been with Christ from the beginning, he could say, when Christ asked if The Twelve would also leave Him, "Lord, to whom shall we go? You have the words of eternal life. We have come to believe and to know that you are the Holy One of God" (John 6:68-69).

Also during this Phase, Jesus issued stronger challenges to the religious establishment, exposing hypocrisy and wrong motives. It became clear for the first time that Jesus was not trying to reform Judaism but starting an entirely new movement. The Jewish leaders became more antagonistic to Jesus, and they developed a plan to kill Him (John 7:1). For the most part, He avoided dangerous places, especially Jerusalem. He even made a trip into the less hostile Gentile regions of Tyre and Sidon (Mark 7:24, 8:10).

By the second half of Phase IV, it was becoming clear that following the Sermon on the Mount in every detail was impossible. Christ's initial call to heart-righteousness no doubt motivated His disciples to live accordingly. But before long, it became clear that they fell far short of this standard. The law tends to affect all believers in this way, at first motivating us to compliance but later discouraging us as we realize our inability to keep it. This causes us to either adapt the law, changing it to conform to our abilities and preferences, or to fall back on the true basis for our acceptance by God: grace working through faith.

All the different events that occurred during this second part of Phase IV created a crisis for Jesus' disciples. They struggled with the call to follow Him. They hadn't expected these latest developments. Things were different now, and they were forced to re-think everything they had been taught growing up in Judaism. What did following the Messiah mean? They were forced to make drastic changes to their temporal, short-sighted worldview. Phase IV is a time of great tension and personal struggle, of crisis and catharsis. And it stretched the disciples' faith at every point.

Sometimes we can structure the circumstances needed for disciples to grow, but often, we can't. As leaders, we too must trust God. Looking to Him to create the circumstances for growth to occur strengthens our faith as disciple builders. Sometimes, we need events that encourage us, and sometimes we need challenging, faith-stretching ones that move us to reevaluate our call and ministry motives. God in His sovereignty provided the situations that caused the first disciples to grow. Jesus' human leadership created many of the specific situations, but His Father was the Architect of the overall application.

As leaders, we too must trust God.

A balance exists between what we do and what God does. If God fails to do His part, we will never complete the task. But He never fails. He has called us to make disciples and assist them as they grow to maturity, and He has made His authority available to achieve His purposes. In Phase IV, disciples need a crisis of faith.

God will bring it about. Be prepared.

Phase V: Deploying Mature Leaders

In this final phase of training, Jesus gave His disciples increasing leadership responsibilities. In addition, He instructed them regarding the priority of servant-leadership, washing their feet to illustrate this truth. They were to love and serve each other even if it meant sacrificing their lives. Ultimately, He commissioned them to go to the whole world with the Good News, discipling others in the same way they had been equipped.

This phase also had two parts. The first focused on developing the overall ministry for the entire community of believers. The second involved yet another difficult time for The Twelve. Ironically, their effective ministry and leadership during the first part of this phase caused their pride to emerge. They needed to be reminded once again that they were incapable, in their own strength, of fulfilling their call and mission. It was only in His strength, carried out through the person of the Holy Spirit, that they would be able to live the Christian life and effectively lead His Church.

Brokenness like this is the hallmark of all true Christian leaders.

Brokenness like this is the hallmark of all true Christian leaders. Our human giftedness and capabilities do not in themselves make us fruitful, although God supernaturally works through the gifts He provides. It's the fruit that's produced by His Holy Spirit that remains, produced through a mature, yielded life in which we've learned to abide in Christ. We learn to trust Him to the point of committing everything into His care.

Once we learn the lessons of brokenness, we're able to produce this fruit. We're able to cast all of our cares and concerns on Him because we know He cares for us (1 Pet. 5:7; Ps. 55:22). This doesn't mean we never stumble but that we've reached a point of maturity in which, after stumbling, we get up, refocus on Christ, and continue to grow till we see Him in death or at His Appearing.

In this phase, Jesus appointed a second group of leaders, The Seventy (Luke 10:1). As we observed earlier, these new leaders were just entering Phase IV, training The Twelve had just completed. We would expect Jesus to repeat the Phase IV themes with this second group, and this is exactly what we find in the Gospel account. So Phase V repeats all the major themes of Phase IV, obviously intended for this new group of leaders.

Christ also gives a new set of instructions for the benefit of The Twelve. But the fact that He repeated what He did in Phase IV for The Seventy was significant for The Twelve as well. As far as they were concerned, He was setting forth a repeatable pattern of sound teaching. He referred to this fact in His Great Commission when He urged His leaders to make new disciples, "teaching them to obey everything I have commanded you" (Matt. 28:20). This is most likely the pattern Paul mentioned to Timothy (2 Tim. 1:13-2:2) and the one we can follow today.

Jesus clearly intended to multiply His leadership as well. In order for that to happen, multiple phases of growth would have to occur all at once. The fact that they did is obvious because of the emergence of The Seventy. In the church today, we can construct a similar, multi-tiered "School of Discipleship," progressive training that presents people mature in Christ.

As mentioned earlier, after Jesus appointed leaders, He spent increasing amounts of time with them. But during this Phase, Jesus began to lessen His involvement with The Twelve. No doubt the ministry grew with the addition of new leaders, and He needed help equipping The Seventy. This required delegating additional responsibilities to The Twelve and probable changes in Jesus' own responsibilities, resulting in less interaction with His closest friends and disciples.

A large movement can become unwieldy without enough middle leaders in place.

Rather than short-circuiting their development, this rite of passage was just what they needed to establish their own independent ministries, a crucial step in the multiplication process. A large movement can become unwieldy without enough middle leaders in place. But when disciple builders conduct the training of Phases IV and V effectively, adequate leaders for future expansion emerge.

Helping Jesus with The Seventy was a new assignment for The Twelve, who progressively advanced in their leadership roles. But these new relationships also increased relational tension, which in turn provided opportunities for maturity (Matthew 18:21). One of the big factors in their spiritual development occurred as Jesus gradually increased their ministry opportunities and responsibilities during each new stage of growth.

Jesus began the equipping of His ministry leaders in Phase III and continued until He left this world at the end of Phase V. At that time, He placed His ministry in the hands of the leaders He developed. They sometimes failed, but they also continued to grow and face challenges, as the Book of Acts testifies. He gave them the same Spirit who had helped Him train them for their leadership roles within the church.

We can and must accomplish this same training today.

We can and must accomplish this same training today. Leadership Development, one of the programs of The 28/20 Project, offers a curriculum that teaches the same progressive themes of Phases III-V. In addition, it offers a Practicum, suggested ministry experiences that help modern disciples apply these leadership principles in everyday life. These experiences occur best in an open, mid-size community that has a focused Gospel mission and is committed to sharing life together in authentic relational connections. This structure (see "Discipleship Community" in Section A of The Appendix) mirrors the house-church model of the Epistles and is a reflection of how Jesus mobilized his leadership corps.

The training in Phase V is vital for the healthy functioning of The Church. Many of the deficiencies we see in the modern church can be linked to a maturity deficit among those in leadership positions. We believe this will change as we reestablish a healthy maturation process.

In the first part of Phase V, Jesus taught many new principles about how the Body of Christ should function. Much of Christ's teaching in this phase came in response to questions brought up by The Twelve. They needed to know how to handle the different problems they encountered as they related to others involved in the ministry. Their leadership responsibilities created situations that challenged their abilities and authority. Jesus used their uncertainty as a teaching opportunity. In fact, most of the principles of servant-leadership can only be fully understood and applied as leaders are forced to grapple with real-life situations.

Reading books and attending seminars are helpful, but only to a point. Relational pressures and spiritual warfare form the crucible for true leadership development. Leaders should help younger leaders develop and engage in ministries based on their spiritual gifts and calling (cf. Eph. 4:11-16). The pressures of relational conflicts and miscommunication shape an environment that forges sacrificial love.

The pressures of relational conflicts and miscommunication shape an environment that forges sacrificial love.

Unfortunately, many modern church leaders, when placed in these crucibles, don't respond in a godly way because they never had the opportunity to mature themselves. Those who work with such leaders must ask God for the faith to exercise patience and grace, gifts of mercy from a merciful God. Sometimes, we must stop following leaders who don't exemplify character and maturity, but only after we've exhibited long-suffering and done our best to help them mature. We do this by trusting the sovereign God who placed them in authority. In the process, we grow as well.

Growth requires experience. In fact, sometimes experience is the only way growth occurs. When we do something new in the Christian life, we tend to rely heavily upon Christ for strength, wisdom, and protection. But as we become more experienced, we also become more confident.

Sometimes confidence is a good thing, inspiring courage and biblical risk-taking. But sometimes it can become counterproductive, causing us to become over-confident, smug and self-sufficient. During this phase of development, this exact thing happened to The Twelve.

Their effectiveness in carrying out their ministry responsibilities eventually backfired as it revealed a hidden weakness: spiritual pride.

It's easy to envision The Twelve as bumbling and ineffective during their time with Jesus. We tend to think of Christ as the Master and The Twelve as more like Abbot and Costello or The Three Stooges. Although it's true that they made mistakes and often held wrong perspectives, they also dispatched successful ministries. They did everything Christ asked, and their training was nearly complete. Because they had successfully participated in the equipping process, endured hardship, and had risen to leadership roles alongside of Jesus, they began to argue among themselves about who was the most effective leader (Luke 22:24).

Two felt they deserved cabinet-level positions in the coming Kingdom, prompting indignant responses from the others. Their pride caused them to misunderstand the true nature of The Kingdom (servant leadership evidenced through sacrificial love) and resulted in one being rebuked as a mouthpiece of Satan (Matt. 16:23). Ironically, their effectiveness in carrying out their ministry responsibilities eventually backfired as it revealed a hidden weakness: spiritual pride.

Does this sound familiar? It should. Too often, the church is characterized by strife and division, instead of unity and peace. I've lost track of all the times I have been guilty of engaging in ego-wars with others in leadership. We all share this malady of egocentricity. (In a group photo, for whom do *you* look first?) We shouldn't be surprised when divisions and arguments occur, but we do need to be aware of the dynamics involved, and respond with maturity.

We must begin by admitting that indwelling sin is the root cause for arguments among believers. James makes this point very clear (James 3:13-4:3). We've become new creatures in Christ (2 Cor. 5:17), and yet sometimes we still argue because we're selfish and allow our earthly nature to sabotage our walk with Christ.

The answer is simple: We must die to our selfish self; put on Christ; live for Him with a new perspective; and in His strength, serve others. In the end, He responds to our obedience by raising us up and giving us the honor we desire (Phil. 2:1-11). But this occurs in His time frame, not ours (1 Pet. 5:6).

Sometimes unresolved pain is the problem in our relational conflicts, making the situation worse. We discuss this in more detail in the next chapter, but the enemy wants to use his lies, born and nurtured during times of woundedness, to make us susceptible to ongoing relational pain in our families, the workplace, and the Church.

The Church desperately needs mature leaders, men and women who are willing to "have the same mindset as Christ Jesus" (Phil. 2:5), considering others more important than themselves (cf. Phil. 2:3). But the evil one wants to divide us, knowing that "If a house is divided against itself, that house cannot stand" (Mark 3:25).

When we rely on ourselves, God disciplines us out of love.

When we rely on ourselves, God disciplines us out of love rather than rebuke us sternly "in order that we may share in his holiness" (Heb. 12:10). As He teaches us, we face and admit our inability to accomplish anything of lasting value without His abiding Presence. He also reminds us of His unconditional love and acceptance. This good pattern yields growth and development. This is what the writer of Hebrews had in mind when he said, "No discipline seems pleasant at the time, but painful. Later on, however, it produces a harvest of righteousness and peace for those who have been trained [discipled] by it" (Heb. 12:11).

Another complicating factor is the role of the evil one and his worldly system of rebellion. Just as he did with Peter, Satan desires to "sift [us] like wheat" (Luke 22:31). The evil one is described later by Peter as "a roaring lion looking for someone to devour" (1 Pet. 5:8).

Peter, who was encouraged by Jesus to strengthen his brothers after he had repented of his own pride, warns us to "Resist him [the evil one], standing firm in the faith, because you know that your brothers throughout the world are undergoing the same kind of sufferings" (1 Pet. 5:8). Peter learned this principle from Jesus after his own experience of failure.

This pattern is repeated throughout the Christian life at all phases of development. God calls us to a difficult task and provides the grace to accomplish it. As we become self-confident, He allows events de-

signed to humble us. Sometimes, God even allows the enemy to attack us (Luke 22:24-32). And He does this because He loves us and
wants us to grow (Heb. 12:4-11; Rom. 8:28-29).

---

*As we become self-confident, He allows events designed
to humble us.*

In the second part of this Phase, Jesus taught about His Second
Coming even as He prepared The Twelve for His departure. And His
death proved essential to the development of their maturity.

At first, this event disoriented them. In spite of the realignment
of their expectations begun in Phase IV, the disciples continued to
hold on to unrealistic perspectives of what His life (and theirs) would
be like while He was on earth. They still hoped for prominent roles
among God's religious elite. Even though He had repeatedly told
them of His imminent death at the hands of the religious establishment, they failed to see it coming. In an ironic twist, the crucifixion
of Christ's body led to the crucifixion of the flesh (pride) of His disciples, which contributed to their maturity (cf. I Cor. 2:1-6).

---

*In an ironic twist, the crucifixion of Christ's body led to
the crucifixion of the pride of His disciples.*

This still occurs today. Modern Christian leaders can develop expectations for how God wants to work in and through them that may
or may not be aligned with God's will. When things don't go as we
planned or hoped, we can become disappointed and discouraged.
And sometimes this leads to bitterness and even the hurt of others

(cf. Heb. 12:11-15).

Scripture asserts that planning and hoping for specific results is not necessarily a bad development: "The mind of man plans his way" (Prov. 16:9a). However, God reserves the right to determine the final outcome: "but the Lord directs his steps" (Prov. 16:9b). As we submit to His agenda, we gain wisdom and learn to rely more and more on His Spirit to enable and guide us. Hardening the heart can lead to stubbornness and the stricter discipline of a Father who loves us (cf. Heb. 12:4-7).

After Christ's crucifixion, His confused, frightened disciples fled and went into hiding. Scripture doesn't tell us everything about this period, but it does reveal their utter disappointment and loss of hope. But once reports of Jesus' resurrection reached them, things began to change. And after He appeared to them, they gained a new perspective. A process of restoration, healing, and transition began. Their hope returned, tempered by wisdom and a new dependence on the Spirit.

This entire situation humbled Jesus' first disciples. They saw their weakness and need for Christ in a new light. It wasn't that they hadn't understood at all, but they had understood only in part. But after these final events of His earthly ministry, they got it. Or at least some of them did.

In the end (or maybe we should say at the new beginning), Jesus had fully prepared them, and He left the ministry in their hands. He gave them The Great Commission, ascended to Heaven and sent the Holy Spirit to live in them, fill them, and provide them with gifts for ministry. However, the Spirit's coming only continued and enhanced what Jesus had begun. These disciples continued the ministry Jesus taught them and spread it all over the world.

In one sense, what occurred at Jesus' death and resurrection and the events leading to Pentecost will never be repeated again. The Spirit will never be sent again by Christ in the same way. There will never again be a Master Disciple Builder like Jesus. Never again will a group of Apostles establish the church and canonize His teachings in Scripture.

What happened to those first disciples happens over and over again.

But in another sense, what happened to those first disciples happens over and over again. Modern believers follow Jesus through His Spirit within us, and He leads us and teaches us. We become active in a community of faith and begin to practice the spiritual disciplines. We learn doctrine, how to share our faith, and have our minds renewed. Many of us become modern apostles, "sent ones" who plant ministries and assume official leadership roles. Almost everyone assumes some kind of leadership: by becoming parents, assuming supervisory roles at work, or being examples of Jesus in our neighborhoods. When disappointments occur, we too can become jaded, self-sufficient, or proud. We, too, need to be reminded of His identity and ours all over again. We need to have our eyes opened again and again until the moment we see Him face to face. Then we will be transformed, perfectly conformed to His likeness (1 John 3:2).

Jesus had a plan and process for helping His people grow to maturity. It involved developing leaders committed to "teaching them to obey everything I have commanded you" (Matt. 28:20a) to subsequent generations of believers.

This pattern of progressive disciple building doesn't prevent struggle. But when problems occur, sound training helps us retain focus and provides perspective, wisdom, and growing maturity. This disciple building experience not only equips us to grow, but it also gives us a platform for helping others grow.

And the process continues.

Chapter 4

Removing Hindrances to Maturity

Unresolved Pain and Uncompleted Developmental Tasks Hinder Growth

The author of the Book of Hebrews admonished his audience to "move beyond the elementary teachings about Christ and be taken forward to maturity" (Heb. 13:5), reminding them that "solid food is for the mature who by constant use have trained themselves to distinguish good from evil" (Heb. 5:14). Later in the epistle, he mentions that in addition to receiving training for maturity, Christ-followers also have a need to eliminate the things that prevent growth. He urged them to "throw off everything that hinders and the sin that so easily entangles. And let us run with perseverance the race marked out for us" (Heb. 12:1). He exhorted them to emulate those who lived by faith and to focus on Jesus, "the author and perfecter of faith" (Heb. 12:2b, NASB; cf. Heb. 5:11-6:3). A mature life is a life of faith.

Considering this, we understand that the process of growth to maturity consists of two parallel components occurring at the same time. The first involves being *trained and equipped* to run the race of faith, following Christ. The second involves *removing the obstacles* that hinder the development of faith.

"Our hands need to be equipped and our hearts need to be restored."

My good friend and colleague, Jack Larson, summarizes this by saying, "Our hands need to be equipped and our hearts need to be restored." [29] We've already observed that this occurs as our minds are renewed. As we grow to maturity, we're able to think (head), feel (heart), and act (hands) like Christ.

In the previous chapter, we discussed the progression of maturity as seen in the equipping process utilized by Christ in the training of The Twelve. Now we want to consider how people can "throw off everything that hinders" (Heb. 12:1) the mature development of faith.

Everyone has spiritual ups and downs. But some Christians face overwhelming obstacles in their growth to maturity. They desire to grow and sincerely apply themselves to the process, but they seem to get stuck, unable to move much beyond their initial faith experience. Some progress at first and then regress. Others experience cycles of spiritual fervor followed by periods of indifference or even rebellion. Some grow but only with great effort and often struggle with depression in the process.

After much prayer and research, we discovered two primary (and often interrelated) reasons for this phenomenon. It may stem from unaddressed or unprocessed pain from an individual's past. Or it may result from the person's inability or lack of opportunity to complete all the developmental tasks that allow for a healthy transition from childhood to adulthood.

Often these two causes work together, creating a complex emotional and relational environment that hampers believers' growth to maturity. This in turn makes it challenging for them to be renewed in the attitude of their minds and put on the new (Christlike) self (cf. Eph. 4:22-24; Rom. 12:1-2). Of course, the evil one inserts his lies and accusations into the process, further complicating matters.

Earlier, we mentioned the maturity that needs to take place in the family of origin. Because there are no perfect families, there's no perfect maturation during this stage of life either. But some homes and families are so dysfunctional that children who grew up there experience crippling problems in adulthood.

As we'll see, God has made provision for imperfect families. He understands that our earthly parents were not able to raise us perfectly, so He has provided a secondary family: the church. This additional family can provide the opportunity for emotional and relational restoration, helping us process past pain and complete the developmental tasks of childhood. Church leaders have a responsibility to understand and apply the dynamics of this restorative process. Regardless, God oversees the process Himself and promises to see it through to fulfillment (Heb. 12:9-10; Phil. 1:6).

Scripture makes it clear: Jesus equipped mature followers who were trained to lead His Church. These were the "men who turned the world upside down" (Acts 17:6 RSV). The contemporary Church needs such leaders. But Christ's ministry involved more than leadership development. It also included helping people heal from the damages of sin.

An effective approach that produces maturity must include both elements: equipping people for strategic leadership and enabling them to recover from emotional and relational damage. And though there's a definite place for clinical therapy, restoration occurs best in the church. People grow and are restored when they receive progressive ministry responsibility while addressing their issues. Such Christians, honest about their sin and struggles but committed to becoming godly, make the best leaders. An end-product will be a grace-filled church culture that welcomes outsiders and accepts sinners because the leaders understand their need for grace.

Jesus' ministry had two related but distinct dimensions. One has to do with preparing us as citizens and leaders in His Kingdom. In the last chapter, we unpacked the five phases of leadership development that Jesus employed in equipping the first disciples to grow to maturity. The second dimension of His ministry centers on our necessity to be restored from the destructive effects of sin. Christ's healing and deliverance ministries underscore this need.

In Luke 3:18, after reading the scroll of Isaiah, Jesus proclaimed the restorative nature of His Kingdom by quoting a text from Isaiah. Isaiah 61:1-4 is of primary importance today for two reasons. By quoting this passage in Luke 4 and citing Himself as the One to fulfill the prophecy, Jesus clearly identifies Himself as the promised Messiah and King of the Jews with authority to redeem and deliver. This passage also sets forth six key aspects of Christ's ministry of redemption and, by implication, how they apply to His Church.

In effect, Jesus was claiming to be the Messiah and, at the same time, describing the nature of His ministry. We should take a closer look at this passage in order to see the significance of His words and how they apply to us as people who need a restoration of our hearts along with an equipping of our hands.

The Messianic passages in the Old Testament fall into two categories. The first emphasizes that the Messiah would come as a "conquering king" or "deliverer." The second describes the Messiah as a "suffering servant" who would suffer and secure redemption for the people of Israel. Ironically, both descriptions refer to Jesus. The role of divine servant describes Jesus in His first coming, and the role of conquering king refers to His second. The Jews did not, as a whole, recognize Christ's first coming and are thus still looking for the Messiah to appear.

> *The role of divine servant describes Jesus in His first coming, and the role of conquering king refers to His second.*

At the time of Christ, the Israelites were weary of foreign dominion. They hadn't experienced political freedom for centuries. After the Babylonian captivity, they struggled with Greek control followed by Roman occupation. No wonder the idea of a Messiah who would appear as a conquering king resonated with them. Unfortunately, this emphasis caused them to minimize His role as suffering servant.

Chapter 61 is one of several passages in Isaiah that describe the Messiah as a "suffering servant." (Others include: Isa. 42:1-4, 49:1-6, 50:4-9, 52:13-53, 53.) The Jews generally applied these passages to themselves as a nation, claiming identity as the suffering servant. But most scholars agree that these passages refer instead to a man often identified as the "Servant of God." This Servant was the Messiah, also appointed to be the mediator of a new covenant, the light of the Gentiles, the salvation of God for the whole world, and the one who would reach this glorious height through servanthood, a service leading to death.

Six Aspects of Christ's Restorative Ministry

In Luke 4:17-21, at the beginning of His ministry, Jesus quoted Isaiah 61:1-4 to both explain and underscore its nature. He concluded by saying, "Today this Scripture is fulfilled in your hearing," indicating, as we will explain, that His ministry was designed at least in part to heal our hearts (emotions) from the damages of sin. In these verses, Jesus mentions six components of His ministry that relate to heart restoration:

1. Proclaim the Good News to the poor

2. Bind up the brokenhearted

3. Proclaim freedom to the captives

4. Proclaim release to the prisoners from the darkness

5. Proclaim the year of the Lord's favor / day of vengeance

6. Comfort all who mourn

The first aspect of Christ's ministry that contributes to restoration from emotional damage is the Gospel message, or Good News. Jesus proclaimed God's love and forgiveness wherever He went, seeking to draw people to Himself for salvation. Becoming a Christian is the most basic element of the restorative process. Non-believers can heal to some degree, but people cannot fully heal until they experience His forgiveness and the new birth He offers.

Lack of forgiveness is a root cause of ongoing feelings of condemnation and hurts the restorative process.

Lack of forgiveness is a root cause of ongoing feelings of condemnation and hurts the restorative process. To experience complete healing, we must receive forgiveness from God, forgive ourselves, and forgive others. Jesus' death and resurrection provide the only real basis for substantial forgiveness.

It is not coincidental that God's offer of forgiveness was at first directed toward the poor. Everyone needs forgiveness, but people who have experienced poverty in any of its forms are usually more aware of that need than those who haven't. The ability to acknowledge and receive forgiveness as a free gift from God through Christ is the starting point for further restoration.

Wounded people need a safe environment where they feel emotionally protected.

The second aspect of Christ's ministry is "to bind up the brokenhearted" (Isa. 61:1b). In this passage, "brokenhearted" refers to people who have been deeply hurt (suffered heart-wounds) and need substantial emotional healing. Taking our hurts directly to Christ promotes healing. He is, after all, a suffering servant who understands wounds (Heb. 4:15-16). But Christ also means for His church to be a place where healing can occur (1 Cor. 12:26). Wounded people need a safe environment where they feel emotionally protected as they express their hurts and receive validation from caring friends. People need to be able to grieve the pain of their past in the presence of their Lord and in fellowship with His people.

The third aspect of Christ's ministry is "to proclaim freedom to the captives." Through His death and resurrection, Christ defeated Satan and set His people free. This liberation affected two dimensions. The first deliverance occurred in the spiritual realm and has a spiritual application. The second occurred in everyday life and has a very practical application.

Scripture mentions things that are "visible" and things that are "invisible" in the Kingdom of Christ (Col. 1:16). A spiritual dimension exists that, although we can't see it with physical eyes, is real and substantial nonetheless. In this spiritual part of the realm, Christ has already set His followers free in a real and dramatic sense. Scripture emphatically asserts that believers have been "delivered from the dominion of Satan and brought into the Kingdom of God" (Col. 1:13). This deliverance means Satan no longer has the legal or moral right to control or condemn the children of God. We may or may not experience this new freedom, but it remains true, and its implications are profound. The Kingdom of God is a place of freedom. We are no longer slaves to sin (Rom. 6:6; John 8:31-36) or captives of the enemy.

Christ has already set His followers free in a real and dramatic sense.

Christ also wants us to experience His freedom in the visible world. It is not enough that we simply understand the truth that the evil one no longer has authority to control and manipulate us, or that indwelling sin no longer dictates our choices. Christ wants us to experience this truth in a real way, adding a practical dimension to this deliverance.

Though legally defeated, Satan continues to exert his control over people, holding them captive in two ways. The first way is through the "devil's schemes" (Eph. 6:11), habitual strategies that we embraced in an attempt to offset the effects of sin. They evolve into addictions and defense mechanisms people use to address unresolved pain.

If we continue to use old mechanisms to deal with our pain rather than rely upon Christ, we remain in bondage to them, to sin, and to the evil one. In the words of Paul, we must learn to "put off your old self, which is being corrupted" (Eph. 4:22b). He reminded them that their old way of thinking was destructive. "So I tell you this, and insist on it in the Lord, that you must no longer live as the Gentiles do, in the futility of their thinking. They are darkened in their understanding and separated from the life of God because of the ignorance that is in them due to the hardening of their hearts" (Eph. 4:17-18). Jesus came to set us free from these unhealthy ways of living. Through His guidance and power we can recognize and replace these harmful practices with more effective and healthy ways of living.

Christ wants to release us from captivity.

But there is a second way the enemy holds us captive. In addition to encouraging addictions that can persist long after people accept Christ, Satan also blinds people to truth, effectively keeping them prisoners in the dark. Christ, however, wants to release us from captivity. Let's examine this fourth aspect of His ministry, "to proclaim release from darkness for the prisoners" (Isa. 61:1c).

Scripture states that Satan has the power to blind unbelievers (2 Cor. 4:4) and does so, effectively preventing them from seeing the truth about Christ and His Kingdom. But salvation removes Satan's power to keep people in the dark. In addition to being set free from the dominion of Satan, we are also set free from the darkness of unbelief. We now have the capacity to see clearly.

But Satan's blinding activities can remain effective even after people become Christians. They occur directly through spiritual attacks and indirectly through a world system of lies that Satan controls until Christ returns. The evil one intends these wicked strategies to confuse and mislead Christians, keeping them away from Christ and in bondage to him. Over time, the strategies evolve into belief systems, strongly-held emotional convictions that shape our view of the world, others, and ourselves. Though believers now have the capacity to recognize these lies, we often fail to do so because we have not "trained (ourselves) to distinguish good from evil" (Heb. 5:14b).

Jesus came to lead us out of the darkness into the light, the truth that sets us free. Part of the process of healing from the damages of sin involves replacing more and more of our wrong beliefs with the truth, thus renewing our minds.

When WDA first studied these verses in Isaiah as a paradigm for promoting emotional healing in the church, we thought the descriptions found there represented the needs of different groups of people who could benefit from different kinds of help. But as we continued to study, we realized that everyone, to some degree, has all these needs. People need various levels of healing in each area.

Everyone needs Christ for salvation, for forgiveness, and for deliverance from sin. Everyone needs to process unresolved pain and learn how to deal with emotions correctly. Everyone needs God's direction and power to deal with the addictions and unhealthy defense mechanisms they use to deal with pain. Some addictions cause obvious harm. Others are not so easily recognized. Still others, such as workaholism and addiction to ministry, may even be applauded at times. And everyone also needs help replacing wrong beliefs with the truth.

Isaiah 61:1-2 describes the restoration Christ brings to all people, and His ministry is designed to provide healing in all the areas the passage mentions. Our research showed these were the same areas that keep people in bondage.

Christ's ministry included a restorative process that heals the damages of sin. During His earthly ministry, He introduced such a process that roughly parallels the early stages of human relational/emotional formation identified by many childhood development specialists. This restorative process is best carried out in a community that imitates many of the dynamics of the family of origin, providing a safe environment for dealing with wounds and reinforcing the tasks associated with healthy development.

We must remember that Jesus does not instantly deliver us from all of the damage we have sustained. He grants forgiveness at the moment of salvation, but some people may take time to fully internalize or appreciate it. Other areas (unresolved pain, addictions, defense mechanisms, and false belief systems) may take even longer to correct. In truth, some of these may be so entrenched that we struggle with them for the remainder of our time on earth.

But for sustained spiritual growth to occur, we must continue to heal from the damages of sin.

The fifth aspect of Christ's ministry is "to proclaim the year of the Lord's favor and the day of vengeance of our God" (Isa. 61:2a). The day will come when Jesus will return to gather His people and reward them for their suffering on His behalf. But He will also dispense wrath to those who rejected Him. Everyone will receive their just reward, either for good or evil (Rom. 2:5-11). Armed with the knowledge that God offers forgiveness but will one day punish all evil enables those who have been hurt to forgive those who hurt them. They realize taking revenge is not their responsibility or prerogative (Rom. 12:19). Only God can right all the wrongs.

Only God can right all the wrongs.

The sixth and last aspect of Christ's ministry is "to comfort all who mourn" (Isa. 61:2b). In itself, mourning is not a pleasant experience. Grieving our losses causes us to feel depressed or sad. But this process is a necessary step in healing us from the damages of sin. God promises to be "a present help in time of trouble" (Ps. 46:1) and a "comfort for people who mourn" (Isa. 61:2). He also promises "to bestow on them a crown of beauty instead of ashes, the oil of gladness instead of mourning, and a garment of praise instead of a spirit of despair" (Isa. 61:3b, c). This describes what happens after people complete the grieving process: they begin to live again. They are able to feel joy (gladness). Their countenance changes (beauty) because they've been released from the stress caused by buried emotions. They want to give praise to their God, which in turn brings Him glory.

The Impact of a Restorative Ministry

When people have experienced significant healing, they are able to grow into healthy, solid believers who help others grow to maturity. The prophet Isaiah calls them "oaks of righteousness, a planting of the Lord for the display of his splendor" (Isa. 61:3). Without restoration, believers can remain crippled and immature, less than what God has designed. This is sad, for all believers can become "oaks of righteousness" and ministers of maturity.

Isaiah goes on to say that those who have been healed in these significant ways and who have grown up will be the ones who will "rebuild the ancient ruins and restore the places long devastated; they will renew the ruined cities that have been devastated for generations" (Isa. 61:4). In other words, these people will have the knowledge, wholeness, and ability to effect healing throughout their culture. They will be able to reverse generations of moral decay and devastation. Through the power of Christ, they will have the ability to reverse the effects of the "sins of the parents to the third or fourth generation" (Ex. 20:5). They will be able to rebuild the culture in a healthy and godly manner, bringing Christ's restorative ministry everywhere they go. They foster revival and renewal for generations to come (Ex. 20:6).

Processing Past Pain

The trauma (pain) that occurs in childhood is often inadequately addressed because the child may not have the support system needed for processing and grieving the difficulties of life. This often results in the development of coping mechanisms. Although these mechanisms help the child survive the trauma of childhood, if carried forward into adult life, they can slow spiritual growth and thus short-circuit maturity.

Church leaders need to understand how past pain can hinder spiritual maturity and devise strategies for helping people experience the restoration of their hearts. In the booklet *How Emotional Problems Develop* (available as a free download from WDA's website, disciple-building.org), Jack Larson explains how childhood trauma affects our ability to grow spiritually and sets forth strategies for processing past pain in order to progress to maturity.

Effective disciple building must include restoration from the effects of these unresolved or unaddressed issues from our past.

Effective disciple building must include restoration from the effects of these unresolved or unaddressed issues from our past. During his time on earth, Christ was concerned about these issues as well. Studying this subject in the Gospels encouraged us to find a built-in restoration process evident in His ministry.

Completing Developmental Tasks

Personal development to maturity, as we've noted, begins in childhood. We need to learn a number of abilities and skills in the area of emotional and relational development during childhood, and the family is the primary training environment where this can occur. Ideally, the culture will also encourage these qualities.

Because of the breakdown of the family and the corresponding deterioration of culture, children often find themselves unable to get what they need. Even in healthier families (those that stay together and are more nurturing), parents are often unable to give their children what they need because, during their own childhood, they never received what they needed. It's difficult to transfer to others what you don't have or communicate concepts you don't understand. And the sad truth is that many parents become so focused on their own needs and survival that they're oblivious to the needs of their children.

The sad truth is that many parents become so focused on their own needs and survival that they're oblivious to the needs of their children.

How the Ministry of Jesus Addressed Childhood Developmental Deficiencies

To help others grow to maturity, we need to be aware of four skills critical for emotional and relational balance that should be developed during childhood. If these skills (often referred to by psychologists as *developmental tasks*) are not adequately completed in the family of origin, they can become a leading cause of spiritual problems later in life. And even if these tasks were completed adequately during childhood, they still need to be reinforced and applied in adulthood.

A healthy church environment is invaluable for reinforcing these skills and helping adults complete any unfinished skills. (For a more complete analysis of this subject, we recommend the book *Changes That Heal* by Dr. Henry Cloud.) There is strong evidence to suggest the progressive disciple building ministry of Christ was intentionally designed to enhance and supplement the emotional development of childhood. Each of the phases discussed in the previous chapter (beginning with Phase II) can be linked with one of the following developmental tasks:

1. Bonding

Bonding is the process by which children from birth to nine months learn to connect with other people who care for them. Through the thousands of interactions that take place between a mother or primary caregiver and her child, the child develops a sense of connection. If all progresses well, the child will see himself as an extension of his mother rather than a separate person. At this stage, a view like this is healthy. Throughout the bonding period, a child normally and naturally internalizes a number of messages, including:

1.   I am loved.
2.   My feelings and needs are OK.
3.   I can trust others to meet my needs.

In these relationships, Jesus revealed His identity, spent much time, and offered His followers grace, acceptance, and hope.

Once he internalizes these messages, the child can start to move away, or separate, from his parents and still believe the messages without the need for constant reinforcement. If bonding does not occur, or if the key messages become distorted or replaced, the child often has problems connecting with others when he becomes an adult. He may not be able to accept love or trust other people. And he may be out of touch with his feelings and needs, thus pushing others away.

This task corresponds to Phase II of spiritual growth: Laying Foundations. Early in His ministry, Jesus gathered a small group of followers and spent the next six to nine months building relationships with them. Establishing this fellowship-community seemed to be His primary emphasis, more important at this time than involving them in outreach. In these relationships, Jesus revealed His identity, spent much time, and offered His followers grace, acceptance, and hope. As mentioned earlier, during this phase of development, the disciples eagerly shared their relationship with Jesus with their friends and colleagues. But though He encouraged these testimonials, Jesus refrained from challenging His followers to assume official ministry responsibilities until they had completed this phase.

Essentially, Jesus and these disciples, as a new family, did what families need to do: they bonded with one another. This new, spiritual family provided an ideal environment for any of His disciples who hadn't completed the developmental task of bonding to do so. It also served to help the new believers address any wounds sustained from inadequate bonding as children.

2. Separation

Separation is the beginning of the process in which children form their own individual identities. Psychologists tell us it happens between the ages of nine months and six years. During this period, children begin to pull away from their parents and experiment with independence. As they become more mobile, they can do more things. If children have internalized the bonding messages, they're able to pull away while still feeling connected and secure.

A person who fails to form a separate and strong sense of identity may face some of the following problems:

- A general lack of self-understanding and direction in life (identity confusion)

- Relational problems such as being too dependent on others, being too isolated from others, feeling too responsible for others, or becoming a caretaker of others

- Significant boundary problems, allowing others to take advantage of and overpower him or taking advantage of and overpowering others [28]

This task corresponds to Phase III of Christian growth: Equipping for Ministry. At the beginning of Phase III, Jesus challenged His disciples to follow Him and learn how to reach out to others (Matt. 4:19). He then took them on a series of evangelistic tours where they ministered alongside Him. They were no longer mere spectators who watched Him serve, as in the previous stage of development. At this phase, they were also actively involved in ministry. In addition, they were beginning to develop their own spiritual identity as part of His Messianic Kingdom. This provided them with incredible esteem.

In the later phases of growth, Jesus continued to expand His disciples' ministry involvement. He allowed them to further develop their ministry abilities, providing them with increasing ownership in God's Kingdom. This helped them define and clarify their spiritual identity and reminded them of how God had uniquely created them to fit into His plans and purposes.

Any of Jesus' disciples who had not yet been able to fully develop a separate identity would have the opportunity to complete this task while learning to minister to others.

Any of Jesus' disciples who had not yet been able to fully develop a separate identity would have the opportunity to complete this task while learning to minister to others. This process began in this phase and continued through the remaining phases of growth.

3. Sorting Out Good and Bad

People who do not complete this task tend to see things as either all good or all bad. For them, everything appears black or white with no shades of gray. However, problems occur because people like this have a hard time tolerating bad in themselves or others. Of course, no one is all good or all bad but a mix of both.

Since the Fall, everything in creation contains this mixture. The Fall marred creation and the image of God in man but did not obliterate His image altogether. The mature Christian must learn to live with this and other tensions. Those who cannot make a balanced distinction and live with the tension between good and bad have not completed this skill. People like this will tend to have one or more of the following problems:

- **Deny the Good in Themselves:** This person has the tendency to blame himself for everything bad that happens, often seeing himself as completely evil and without hope. He denies his worth and/or ability to contribute anything good. He may elevate others, believing they're better than he is, or be critical of others, judging them as equally evil. Depression and isolation often accompany this position.

- **Deny the Bad in Themselves:** This person cannot tolerate the idea that he's ever wrong because it's the equivalent of admitting he's wholly evil and therefore worthless. He must doggedly deny the existence of bad in himself, blaming others for anything bad or disappointing while justifying himself. This person has great difficulty acknowledging his faults. He's so difficult to be around that he often has few friends or colleagues.

- **All Good to All Bad:** This person tends to see people and situations as "all good" at first, but after experiencing problems, he sees the same people and situations as "all bad." As a result of this distortion, he initially views a new relationship, church, or job as perfect. But once the inevitable problems occur, he switches his assessment to "all bad" and seeks to remove himself or others from the situation. Often, he keeps changing relationships, churches, and jobs in a search for the perfect situation. The truth is that people and situations are both "good and bad" at first, and "good and bad" later. But it's difficult for him to see this reality.

The truth is that people and situations are both "good and bad" at first, and "good and bad" later.

This developmental task corresponds to Phase IV: Developing New Leaders. Jesus launched this phase of growth by preaching The Sermon on the Mount. He explained to those who had been appointed as new leaders what He expected of them in terms of inner righteousness. In fact, He raised the bar of righteousness so high that no one could reach the moral standards He set. That was His way of forcing them to wrestle with their inability to keep the law as He defined it.

The Sermon drove the new leaders to sort out the tension between good and bad and come to realize a deeper meaning and application of grace. And it accomplishes the same thing in the hearts of modern-day disciples.

During this phase, Jesus also began to expose the legalistic and hypocritical practices and attitudes of the Pharisees and scribes. These "blind guides" (Matt. 23:24) claimed to keep the Law but were miserable failures. The Apostles had to accept the fact that no one could keep the Law completely, but everyone still needed to try. They had to accept the idea that they could sin less but never be sinless.

In addition, there was a dramatic rise in the persecution Jesus and His followers were experiencing. All of this continued to cause the Apostles to reevaluate their expectations of the Christian life. They had to come to grips with the fact that they were both good and bad. No matter how much progress they made against sin, they would remain both good and bad until the final Resurrection. They also needed to accept the fact that the entire fallen world was never going to accept Jesus and be changed. The spiritual battle they had entered was not going to go away. They could make an impact, but until the return of Christ, Satan would remain the ruler of this world.

Jesus' disciples grew up in a culture that taught the Law and its requirements and offered a system of atonement. In the Christian life, all the concerns surrounding our struggles with sin come to the surface again and again. This phase of development helps us deal with our sin more completely and with more grace.

I'm convinced this is one of the markers of maturity most lacking in many evangelical churches. We struggle to sort out and apply grace and truth because we can't accept that we're all both good and bad. We all need to repent and receive His grace and forgiveness again and again. This is the good news of the Gospel that both justifies and sanctifies. Churches should be places where no perfect (i.e. "all good") people reside so that they can become places where sinners, (not "all bad" people, but fellow disciples in need of sanctification) can feel loved and accepted. And for this to occur, we must mature.

4. Gaining Independence and Functioning as Mature Adults

This last developmental task usually occurs during late adolescence. It happens when a child moves from a dependent relationship with his parents and other adults (a situation where he has limited authority, freedom, and choice), to a more equal relationship with these people. This process happens slowly and should be completed as the child leaves home, moves out on his own, and takes total responsibility for his own life.

But some people never complete this task. They remain dependent on their parents and other adults. As a result, they continue to feel less mature than other adults. There seems to be an increasing number of young men and women in Western culture who still reside with their parents long after they should have left home.

If this developmental task is not completed, several of the following characteristics are usually present: an inordinate need for approval and/or fear of disapproval, a crippling fear of failure, a need for permission to be given before initiating action, strong feelings of inferiority, a loss of power or control (which is often given away to others), an over-dependence on others, an idealization of people in authority, an inability to respectfully submit to God's established authorities, and bitterness or helplessness from feeling trapped as children in an adult world.

This task corresponds to Phase V: Developing Mature Leaders. During this period of time, Jesus appointed a second group of leaders, The Seventy (Luke 10). By this time, The Twelve were helping Him lead this new group of leaders as they continued to reach out to new groups of unreached people. Jesus, because He was doing much more work with The Seventy, began to withdraw from The Twelve while at the same time giving them more authority. The result was that The Twelve developed more independence from Jesus as their earthly leader and gained more confidence in the ministry.

However, as mentioned earlier, this success created other challenges. As The Twelve worked through these struggles, they ultimately gained the ability to attain a new level of maturity. At the end of this period, Jesus left and went back to heaven, leaving these mature leaders in charge of His Church.

This process represents exactly what is needed for people to become mature adults. As we've repeatedly observed, these are the kinds of leaders the Church needs today. Leaders need to be able to understand their authority and exercise it appropriately. They need to establish their independence and take responsibility for their lives so they can assume healthy responsibility for others. They need to come out from under old authority relationships and establish new ones in which they can operate as peers with other leaders, establishing an equal role with those in authoritative positions alongside them. Only as they complete this task are they able to show proper respect for and submission to the authorities God places over them.

Leaders need to be able to understand their authority and exercise it appropriately.

In the same way Jesus' ministry allowed any of His disciples who had not yet completed the task of becoming an adult to do so, the modern church needs to give disciples time to mature. We must also make sure people have matured to the point that this challenge is appropriate lest we put them in jeopardy as Paul warned against in 1 Timothy 3:6. Appointment to leadership should be an opportunity for people to establish their independence and gain equal authority with other adults, thus making them more effective for the future in both the church and the home.

We Need Better Parenting Skills

Churches training parents in strategies that would help them pass on healthy styles of relating to their children would help the overall goal of producing mature, responsible believers. Parents of younger children would benefit especially, since this approach could prevent some of the problems we've mentioned. In addition, creating a progressive disciple building process for young, single adults in the church would help ensure this outcome.

Another benefit of this process would occur as parents grew to maturity and addressed their emotional and relational needs. The resulting maturity would filter down through the family and provide a better atmosphere for dealing with issues both parents and children face.

Fortunately, there are a number of things the church can do to make families healthier. These include developing strategies for appropriately empowering our children, teaching them how to deal with negative emotions, teaching them how to grieve and have a balanced approach to forgiveness, and teaching them how to stand up for themselves in healthy ways. In this way, we can create balanced support systems by giving our children healthy views of themselves, the world, and God.

Restorative growth heals and empowers, transforming lives.

Healing from emotional and relational damage takes time, but people who address these issues find significant improvement, including growth in their walk with God. Restorative growth heals and empowers, transforming lives. Unfortunately, some people are so damaged that, even if we provide the support they need, they will have trouble growing spiritually. At first, people like this may have to focus almost exclusively on emotional recovery. Eventually, they'll grow in other ways, but only with proper care. Some disciples may require the help of a professional counselor. But most people will recover from the damage of the past if we can incorporate restorative growth into a biblical disciple building process.

Other WDA publications discuss the topic of disciple building and emotional health more thoroughly than this one. Listed below are emotional-restorative goals addressed during the Five Phases. (For a more complete discussion of this dynamic and for help in addressing the hindrances to maturity, visit us at: http://www.disciplebuilding.org/ministries/restorative-ministry/.)

Phase I: Establishing Faith

1. Understand and receive forgiveness.

2. Begin a relationship with God.

3. Learn how to repent and trust God.

Phase II: Laying Foundations

1. Identify and correct distorted views of God.

2. Develop healthy self-awareness.

3. Feel part of a community group.

4. Understand a biblically balanced view of man.

5. Develop personal responsibility.

6. Understand addictive behavior.

7. Identify and learn to deal with emotions appropriately.

8. Understand grieving and forgiveness.

9. Identify personal needs and appropriate ways to meet them.

10. Understand how the past affects the present.

11. Learn to trust God and safe people.

Phase III: Equipping for Ministry

1. Understand and apply the power of personal choice.

2. Develop a healthy perspective on limits.

3. Identify and overcome personal fears related to relationships and ministry.

4. Develop healthy relationships and relationship skills.

5. Learn to initiate in healthy ways toward others.

6. Learn to take responsibility for personal problems and not the problems of others.

7. Learn to address conflict appropriately.

8. Develop comfort with and the ability to be one's true self.

9. Feel accepted and loved by God, not condemned.

10. Become more aware of strengths and weaknesses.

11. Learn to balance time for self and others.

12. Develop the ability to avoid compromising the truth.

13. Feel connected to others.

14. Begin to identify personal spiritual gifts and passion.

Phase IV: Developing New Leaders

1. Learn healthy team and family dynamics.

2. Develop negotiation and problem-solving skills.

3. Develop self-control and flexibility (not too rigid or too lax).

4. Adopt the perspective that to struggle and fail is human.

5. Become a contributing member of a leadership team.

6. Accept the idea that people and institutions contain both good and bad characteristics.

7. Learn to appropriately subordinate oneself to a group.

8. Grow in the ability to be a servant leader.

9. Develop the ability to address and alleviate relational problems.

10. Be able to clarify and focus spiritual gifts and passion.

11. Develop realism (not overly critical or obsessive).

12. Understand the complexity of human problems and solutions.

13. Understand that truth often lies in tension with other truth.

14. Understand that suffering is normal and is designed to produce good.

Phase V: Developing Mature Leaders

1. Develop skills to lead a ministry team and/or a family.

2. Develop a personal ministry based on individual passion and calling.

3. Learn to appreciate the differences between people and the contribution each makes.

4. Develop a vision of how a team ministry can change the world.

5. Learn that effective teams come from everyone doing their part.

6. Learn that effective teams accomplish more than the sum of their parts.

7. Learn to allow eternal matters and world vision to impact priorities and decisions.

8. Learn to determine God's will in a team setting.

9. Learn that God can supply all a team needs to accomplish His will.

Chapter 5

The Church is God's Plan A

(There is no Plan B.)

Growth to maturity occurs best in the local church where mature leaders construct practical programs that develop other mature leaders, who can in turn help others, thus continuing the process.

People who want to help others grow know they must depend on God for help, but they also realize He expects them to assume responsibility and take initiative. Whether the leader is a college student in a campus ministry, a community group leader, a pastor, or a parent, when it comes to helping people mature, questions arise, such as:

- Where do I begin?

- How do I know what someone really needs?

- Is there a way of tracking spiritual maturity?

- Is there a growth process?

- What causes growth to occur?

- How do I help someone take the next step?

- What if I run into problems?

- What materials should I use, and where can I find them?

  - Are they appropriate for this person?

  - Are they practical?

  - Are they affordable?

  - Is there a way to provide structure without rigidity?

As we've seen, Scripture reveals a process of growth to maturity in Christ. Though mysterious in some ways, it's also practical and manageable for those who want either to help others grow or to grow themselves. We're all unique, but we all grow. Although every child is different, they all develop in similar ways, growing in stages and needing nourishment and care.

In the same way, spiritual children are unique, and they, too, grow up gradually. They all progress according to God's prescribed stages of development (Heb. 5:12-14; 1 John 2:12-14). But like natural development, spiritual growth can be stunted or delayed without proper care.

Again, Jesus had a plan for building mature leaders. He equipped them, addressed the obstacles that hindered their growth, and commissioned them to do the same for others. But we need to remember that these leaders fulfilled His commission by planting churches. Disciple building that produces maturity takes place in the church. The Church is God's Plan A. There is no Plan B.

This doesn't mean that parachurch organizations such as WDA

aren't strategic in disciple building efforts. Seminaries, Bible schools, and denominational and interdenominational missions are of vital importance. Most scholars believe these are part of the Church as extensions of local churches or coalitions of churches, and we agree. But we also believe maturity occurs best in spiritual community, overseen by skilled leaders. For this reason, local churches must be mobilized and equipped to help people grow to maturity. Once again, Christ's ministry can serve as a template.

Maturity is Intentional, Supported By Five Initiatives

After Christ left earth, He sent the Spirit to help His followers continue to mature, reminding them of truths He had taught and leading them to additional insights about Him and His Kingdom. This process occurs in the local church as leaders implement initiatives that encourage maturity and believers grow in unity and community. The gracious enabling of a sovereign God makes this both possible and effective. Paul referred to this balance of human initiative and God-orchestrated results when he reminded the Corinthians that he and Apollos planted and watered, but God caused the growth (1 Cor. 3:6).

The Gospel of grace that launched our Christian lives is the same Gospel of grace that sustains us.

Apart from the grace of God, no spiritual life is possible: "For by grace you have been saved through faith—and this not from yourselves, it is the gift of God—not by works so that no one can boast" (Eph. 2:8-9). The Gospel of grace that launched our Christian lives is the same Gospel of grace that sustains us. "As you received the Lord

Jesus, so walk in Him" (Col. 2:6). God is the One who causes spiritual growth, but He entrusts us with the task of disciple building as a critical part of the process.

There's a partnership between church leaders and God that brings about maturity. People who want to help others grow need to understand the progression of spiritual maturation and employ God's divinely-ordained initiatives (means of grace) to facilitate growth ("I planted the seed, Apollos watered it, but God has been making it grow" – 1 Cor. 3:6). Understanding how the partnership works is an important factor in enabling growth to maturity. Church leaders need to be able to identify a disciple's phase of growth and employ the proper initiative to facilitate development at each point of spiritual maturity.

Once again, we can benefit by studying the approach of Jesus. Under the power and guidance of the Spirit, He repeatedly engaged in five activities (growth initiatives) to help His disciples mature:

- He built **relationships** with them, connecting appropriately and strategically.

- He taught them **content** (truth about God and His Kingdom) and trained them in skills they would need in ministry.

- He provided **accountability**, encouraging them to put truth into practice.

- He spent time in **prayer** for them, often fighting spiritual battles on their behalf.

- He placed them in **situations** that challenged them to greater commitment and faith.

Modern disciple builders can employ the same initiatives Christ used. Only God the Holy Spirit can effect growth, but we can work in step with Him to facilitate and support growth that leads to maturity.

Everything Begins with Relationship

Relationships lie at the heart of helping others mature. Jesus was *with* His men. He loved them, exhorted them, and took them with Him. "Come and see," and "Follow me!" were His invitations to discover who He was in everyday life.

Modern disciples also need someone who loves them.

Modern disciples also need someone who loves them. They often arrive in the church with hurt feelings, wounded hearts, and disillusionment. They may feel no one cares enough to relate to them, help them deal with their struggles, or train them to grow up in the faith. Unless people know we care, they won't trust us enough to listen to what we say. Like Jesus, we must spend time with people if we hope to impact their lives.

Someone said children spell love *t-i-m-e*. This also holds true for spiritual children. Accountability without love will frustrate and eventually fail. Often what affects others most is not what we say but how we live and relate.

In our fast-paced world, relationships are easy to neglect. We may be tempted to think we can influence others by dumping information on them. But building solid men and women of God requires more than that. Growing mature disciples requires relationships. This takes time and effort but pays greater dividends overall. Through caring relationships, we can make a real difference in others' lives.

Leaders must be wise and consistent, sacrificing in the short term to establish fruit that will remain and, in time, reproduce. An emphasis on evangelism without relational, accountable disciple building is an incomplete approach to fulfilling the Great Commission. This won't be easy to correct, but if we begin now, we can address deficiencies and build for the future.

Many younger adults are both suspicious of tradition and hungry for relational connection. So our approaches must aim at creating authentic, caring community with no appearance of manipulation or recruitment. Such a change will require a change in our thinking, our priorities, and perhaps our structures, but the result will be a new generation of church leaders who champion true maturity.

As we explored the ministry of Jesus, we saw that He modeled truth before He taught it. He then worked alongside His disciples to teach them skills, making sure they understood before giving further responsibilities. Next, He allowed them to undertake ministry activities without His presence. Eventually, He left them to perform tasks without Him and expected them to handle matters as mature followers.

We call this process of gradually training another person by changing the nature of the relationship and the leader's involvement in the process the OPSI Steps of Transfer, derived from an acronym for the four stages of transference:

1. Observation: They observe as *we do it.*

2. Participation: They participate in the activity *with us.*

3. Supervision: We allow *them* to do it, and we oversee the activity, providing feedback.

4. Independence: They accomplish the activity *entirely on their own,* apart from us.

In effective disciple building, this process often repeats itself. Nearly every new skill requires some application of the OPSI Steps of Transfer. In order for the process to work, however, modeling is critical. For this reason, disciple builders must be prepared to do the work of the ministry alongside those we train. Handing out manuals is not enough. We must do ministry together.

But modeling is only part of the relationship. Disciples must know we care, that we love God and love them. And this love must be real. Superficial or artificial relationships fool no one. The Scriptures exhort us, "Let your love be without hypocrisy" (Romans 12:9a, NASB). People can often sense the difference between a ministry-based relationship and genuine concern.

Only Christ can give us the ability to love sacrificially. And this is the purpose-driven goal of disciple building that produces maturity. "The goal of this command is love, which comes from a pure heart and a good conscience, and a sincere faith" (1 Tim. 1:5). Paul also reminded his disciples, "As apostles of Christ we could have been a burden to you, but we were gentle among you, like a mother caring for her children. We loved you so much that we were delighted to share with you not only the Gospel of God but our lives as well, because you had become so dear to us" (1 Thess. 2:7-8).

This kind of love is not natural, but supernatural, empowered by the Holy Spirit. If we want to help others, we must grow as well. As we do, we will become like Christ, willing to lay down our lives for others. Jesus summed it up, "All men will know that you are My disciples if you love one another" (John 13:35) and "Greater love has no one than this, that one lay down his life for his friends" (John 15:13).

Content is Critical for Growth

The Scriptures testify that the Word of God is powerful, setting us free from sin, enabling us to walk uprightly before God, and equipping us for every good work. Disciples need instruction in the Word of God. We must instruct them faithfully and patiently, pointing out promises, principles, and the characteristics and attributes of a good God who loves them. We must teach and train them in spiritual warfare and the skills of ministry. Young disciples need to learn theology and how to understand and study the Bible, its source. They need to know about mankind and the redemption of the Cross. The list is long and complicated. Teaching content is central to the disciple building process, because truth changes people (Rom. 12:1-2).

Growth occurs when truth does its work in us.

But truth learned in a vacuum never transforms. Growth occurs when truth does its work in us. Truth that changes must be incorporated into all of life. It is not enough only to hear a good sermon, meditate on a passage of Scripture, or read a good book. Even a firm hold on a theological position won't transform our hearts or behavior. (Some of the most un-Christlike people have the best doctrine.) In order for truth to set us free or allow us to help others, we must obey it.

For this reason, we must design our teaching with application in mind. This approach requires more than lectures or reading lists. We must consider the agents and structures that facilitate the doing of truth and develop training, community group studies, growth projects, and theological concepts that encourage application. Driven by relationships and prayer, this curriculum should be built on the premise that true growth occurs gradually and progressively with appropriate accountability as a hallmark. Truth must be taught in such a way that people can absorb and apply it.

Accountability is Required

Jesus made it clear: "Teach them to obey everything" (Matt. 28:20). As every parent knows, mere communication of concepts is not enough. We must teach truth so a disciple will obey it. This requires patience, wisdom, and accountability or, as the Bible calls it, "admonition" (Col. 1:28-29). In order for truth-teaching that produces obedience to occur, we must design some type of supervisory structure and process in which we can observe whether or not a disciple is doing what Christ commanded. We must also put relational pressure points in place that encourage obedience.

I once had a boss who said, "It's not what you *expect* but what you *inspect* that matters." Unfortunately, we live in a day when any form of inspection is viewed as meddling or (worse) controlling. To avoid the perception of wrongly interfering in a disciple's life, we must understand appropriate boundaries and learn to make wise assessments for each disciple. Wisdom in discernment requires some type of measurement.

Don't Damage the Fruit!

The evening youth meeting was packed with teenagers, many of whom had never entered the church before. Most came from the bad part of town. They sat in the back: hard, bitter, suspicious. But the live music, entertaining speaker, and caring authenticity of the student ministry had attracted them. As the message shifted from popular culture to the Christian life, you could sense the Spirit working. Some came forward weeping, and others shifted in their seats, nervous as they considered Christ's life and claims.

Finally, one young man bolted for the door. I recognized him. I'd spoken to him earlier when we canvassed the community to invite people to the event. I followed him into the summer night.

As we talked together, I could see he was struggling to understand and longed to believe. But an abusive father and life on the streets had left him suspicious and jaded. He was angry but willing to talk. I sensed no one had ever loved and accepted him. He felt weak, alone, and confused.

As we spoke about Christ and the life He offered, he lit a cigarette in an attempt to quiet his jangled nerves. I was about to suggest that we pray together, asking God for answers, when one of the adult leaders approached. I was stunned when I heard the scathing rebuke:

"Put out that cigarette right now or get off this property! We don't allow smoking here. Our bodies are temples of the Holy Spirit!" The young man crushed out the cigarette as instructed and turned away. As he left, I offered an awkward explanation, but our moment had passed. I never saw him again.

At first, I was angry at my fellow church leader. One abrupt exhortation, and all the work and prayer invested in reaching that young man were wasted. Later, I realized the church leader was also trying to be faithful and hold others accountable to the Word as he understood it. It wasn't as if I liked smoking, a habit that had recently killed my mother. But that wasn't the point.

In this case, well-intended accountability was misplaced. True accountability must be driven by proper assessment of needs and fueled by genuine love, both by-products of a caring relationship. That night, dealing with the smoking habit wasn't my young friend's primary need. Instead, he craved love, acceptance, and grace. He desperately wanted to see the kindness of God, which in turn leads to repentance (Rom. 2:4). Sooner or later, we would have discussed smoking, but only after a solid spiritual foundation had been laid. And maybe we wouldn't have needed to discuss it at all. The Spirit often prompts young believers to abandon old habits.

As Western culture deteriorates, unbelievers are adopting more destructive lifestyle choices. To combat this trend, Christians must be full of grace and truth, "meeting people where they are, helping them take the next step." One person might be able to abandon a particular sin at the moment of conversion, but another might struggle with the same sin for years. Deliverance from habitual sin often requires relational support, wisdom, and prayer. The level of accountability we offer must be in sync with the Spirit of God, and we must be prepared to engage in spiritual warfare to pull down any existing strongholds.

This is where the Good News is really Good News. The Gospel both justifies and sanctifies. When Paul is confronted with the reality that he's unable to live a sin-free life in "this body that is subject to death" (Rom. 7:24), he's also comforted by remembering that "there is now no condemnation for those who are in Christ Jesus, because through Christ Jesus the law of the Spirit who gives life has set you free from the law of sin and death" (Rom. 7:21-8:4).

Church leaders need wisdom to live in the tension of knowing when and how to exhort people to be set free from certain sins and knowing when and how to provide continuing support as they struggle against these same sins. Scripture urges us to encourage one another daily so that no one is hardened by the deceitfulness of sin (Heb. 3:13). But God's Word also instructs us to bear each other's burdens (Gal. 6:2). Grace accepts people where they are but also urges them not to stay there.

If we intend to help people grow, accountability (assessment, affirmation, and recognition of needs) to the truth must continue throughout the maturation process. And this must be wise accountability, the kind Paul had in mind when he said, "He is the one we proclaim, admonishing and teaching everyone *with all wisdom*, so that we may present everyone fully mature in Christ" (Col. 1:28, emphasis added).

Jesus, once again, is our example. He wasn't afraid to get tough when the situation called for it. He overturned the tables of the money-changers, He rebuked Peter for falling under Satan's influence (Mark 8:33), and He told the woman caught in adultery to "go now and leave your life of sin" (John 8:11).

But when the situation called for it, Jesus was also patient and forgiving. After Peter denied Him, Christ reinstated His wayward disciple. Jesus also refused to condemn the woman caught in adultery. Before leaving Earth, He promised to send another like Himself (John 14:15-18), referring to the Holy Spirit. The Spirit is also called "the Helper" (Greek *paraklesis*, "One who comes alongside to help and encourage").

Do you see? God sent Jesus to put His arm around our shoulder and provide support. He's Someone we can lean on. In the same way, disciple builders must become "alongsiders," life coaches who walk with the Spirit and encourage maturity by providing appropriate accountability.

Prayer Causes Growth to Occur

Earlier, we discussed the training that occurred during Phase V, the period of Jesus' ministry when the disciples struggled with pride and self-sufficiency. At this time, Jesus revealed to Peter that the devil was intent on attacking him. He then went on to say, "But I have prayed for you" (Luke 22:32).

Jesus prayed constantly. He prayed all night before He selected The Twelve (Luke 6:12). He prayed after feeding the 5000, where Scripture tells us the disciples needed clearer understanding of who Christ was and how He operated "for they had not understood about the loaves; their hearts were hardened" (Mark 6:52).

When The Twelve encountered the storm at sea, Jesus was on the land, praying.

When The Twelve encountered the storm at sea, Jesus was on the land, praying. The account says, "and seeing them straining at the oars... He came to them, walking on the sea" (Mark 6:48, NASB). He prayed, lifting His eyes to heaven before raising Lazarus from the dead (John 11:38-44). The Bible contains multiple references to Jesus, the Master Disciple Builder, praying.

And He's still doing the same thing. Hebrews 7:25 reminds us that Jesus, our High Priest, "is able to save completely those who come to God through Him, because he always lives to intercede for them." In another place, Scripture reminds us that both Christ and the Holy Spirit intercede for us continuously (Rom. 8:26,34).

Jesus also exhorted His disciples to pray and not lose heart. He understood prayer as an element of spiritual warfare, essential for successful ministry. He reminded His disciples that before entering the strong man's house and plundering his goods, they must bind him (Mark 3:27). He pointed out that agreement in prayer on earth gives believers authority in the heavenly realms (Matt. 12:28-29, 16:17-19). In Ephesians 6 the Apostle Paul reminds us to put on the armor of God and pray, standing together in unity (cf. Eph. 4:3; Phil. 2:1-4; 1 Tim. 2:1-8). In addition to warfare prayer, Jesus also prayed for insight, protection, provision, and sovereign intervention. He prayed early in the morning and throughout the day.

Prayer is the disciple building initiative most challenging to implement and most often neglected.

Paul reminds us that teaching doctrine isn't enough. After a passage in his letter to the Ephesian church filled with wonderful insight regarding God and His Kingdom, Paul says, "I pray also that the eyes of your heart may be enlightened" (Eph. 1:18). I believe prayer is the disciple building initiative most challenging to implement and most often neglected, in part because we hate admitting that anything is beyond our control. By definition, prayer represents our willingness to acknowledge that we need God to intervene, to do the impossible. But spiritual warfare also makes prayer difficult. Satan, who hates it when we pray, understands the power of intercession.

We should encourage our disciples to pray, and we should pray with them. As with every other disciple building initiative, the prayer needs change as a disciple grows. I'm always amazed at the prayers of young believers, who ask God for the craziest things. But even more amazing is that He often answers these zany requests.

But this shouldn't surprise us. God is intent on showing young believers that He loves them and they can trust Him. For this reason, He often answers the prayers of a less mature Christian in different ways than He responds to the prayers of someone more mature. Therefore, we must understand how prayer changes through the phases of growth.

Structured Growth Situations

Jesus spoke of the importance of structures to accomplish the goals of the Kingdom. His admonition to put wine in the proper container is as important today as in the first century. Whether in a home, on the road, or in the Temple, Jesus continuously instructed His small band of disciples. His goal was clear: to equip them for the leadership of the church, which included reproducing themselves through others. Jesus trained the first church leaders in a dynamic school centered around relationships and taught truth in the context of real-life situations.

Jesus' goal was clear: to equip them for the leadership of the church, which included reproducing themselves through others.

Modern Christian educators have tended to neglect the relational model of leadership development. Instead, they've chosen an approach that communicates most content in the classroom. This model is derived more from Greek academic approaches to learning than the classic rabbinical model that Christ followed. An academic education has its advantages, and as we will see, Jesus sometimes used an instructional format. But we must recognize that the classic academic model is not configured to instruct in the context of real-life situations. Although valuable as a means of imparting information and technical skills, the classroom doesn't do as good a job as the relational model in training character and conduct, the primary goals of Christian development and maturity. Recognizing the limits of the academic approach, many Christian educational institutions are now attempting to adopt more relational methods, but the classroom/lecture method still prevails.

Unfortunately, the training structure favored in academia has become the prototype for most local churches.

Unfortunately, the training structure favored in academia has become the prototype for most local churches. Though some contemporary small groups are recovering the concept of micro-community, many still function like classrooms, with little opportunity for relational interaction and almost no opportunity to go "outside the walls" and engage the culture. The result is that people are instructed but not held relationally accountable to put the truth they learn into practice, and concepts are seldom modeled. It's time to adopt a more comprehensive approach that integrates several types of structures to better accomplish the goal of applying and not merely understanding truth.

The disciple builder must recognize two different kinds of situations for growth. Sometimes life-events go far beyond our control. These are God-ordained circumstances. When these occur, the role of a wise disciple builder is to understand and cooperate with what God has planned and help the disciple respond in faith.

But other types of situations can be planned or constructed by the disciple builder to create a faith-building experience for the disciple. At WDA, we refer to these constructed situations as *structures*. Thus, when the disciple builder plans a specific event and challenges the disciple to be a part of it, he has created a structure for disciple building that leads to maturity.

When used this way, the term structures includes all the activities used by church leaders to plan and organize a growth environment that facilitates the maturation process. All the meetings, programs, activities, and scheduled events that make up the calendar of the disciple are structures. These events may be as simple as an appointment over coffee with a friend or as complex as a community-wide program lasting several days or more. But they are all intentional, considered, and planned by leaders who desire to create opportunities for growth and development. The leadership has the responsibility to construct these structures as part of a complete disciple building regimen.

Leadership has the responsibility to construct these structures as part of a complete disciple building regimen.

Six distinct types of structures form the framework for spiritual life and development. Five of these should be incorporated into the scheduled activities of a local community of believers. The sixth should be incorporated into the ongoing spiritual disciplines of an individual disciple.

- Discipleship Communities

- Life-Coaching Relationships

- Public Gatherings

- Ministry Activities

- Instructional Formats

- The Spiritual Disciplines (Habits of the Heart)

Although each element is unique, when taken together, they all play an important role in our spiritual development. The best arrangement for Christian growth occurs when all these structures work in concert. And both structured and unstructured situations are essential in a disciple's development. Both create opportunities for growth. This was what Paul had in mind when he asserted in Romans 8:28-29, "that in all things God works for the good" of those who are being "conformed to the image of His Son."

The best arrangement for Christian growth occurs when all these structures work in concert.

Architecture for Growth to Maturity

Acronyms are an effective educational tool. When I was learning to fly a small plane, my instructor suggested that before every landing, I review the procedures using the G.U.M.P. method (Gas, Undercarriage, Mixture, Propeller). I was grateful for this little tip, because on one occasion it saved me a great deal of embarrassment and possible injury when I almost forgot to put my landing gear down on final approach. In the same way, I use the acronym **R-CAPS** to remember the growth initiatives mentioned above: **R**elationships, **C**ontent, **A**ccountability, **P**rayer, and **S**ituations. **R-CAPS** also serves as a reference for planning projects that promote maturity.

Understanding how spiritual growth occurs enables leaders to stay in step with the Spirit by anticipating the normal process of development God has created. There's room for our wise planning alongside His sovereign initiation and control. By focusing on what to teach, how to relate, and how to pray for the disciples according to their level of maturity, we don't over or under-challenge them. Instead, we meet them where they are and help them take the next step. The programs used are not formulas, but individually designed to help people grow to Christlike maturity within a church's loving community. They're strategically crafted to accommodate individuality and achieve specific outcomes.

We meet them where they are and help them take the
next step.

Rather than being rigid, this approach allows us to modify what we do to help a disciple grow based on her changing needs while allowing for progression toward the goal of maturity. The entire process of spiritual growth is dynamic, requiring critical, strategic thinking and constant dependence on the Spirit to reveal helpful ways to encourage and build faith. The complexities of our human nature and the dynamics of the Christian life require these kinds of strategic adjustments.

The alternatives to a flexible progression that allows room to address unique needs are either to abandon flexibility for a one-size-fits-all program or to abandon progressive development and attempt to meet whatever need seems most urgent at the time. Although our more fluid approach to discipleship involves more consideration and planning than others, when it comes to encouraging maturity, it achieves amazing results. What's easy isn't always best. And what's best is not always difficult to implement. It just requires forethought and strategic planning.

R-CAPS

Once we understand the specific growth initiatives (R-CAPS) Jesus used to stimulate growth and the progressive pattern of sound teaching (five phases) He followed, we can construct a grid-architecture that assists us in helping someone else grow. This framework of spiritual development, which we refer to as the R-CAPS Grid, is a helpful and practical tool for helping people grow to maturity. By using this framework, Life Coaches can prayerfully design individual growth projects that, under the power of the Spirit, help disciples grow to maturity. The R-CAPS Grid has also been helpful in crafting discipleship programs that help local churches build disciples.

This framework of spiritual development is a helpful and practical tool for helping people grow to maturity.

The R-CAPS Grid is straightforward and simple, yet not simplistic. When we understand the process, petition God for wisdom, and use the tools given us by the Spirit of God to facilitate growth, we can effectively help people grow to maturity. We accomplish this by tracking the five progressive phases of spiritual growth and integrating these with the five growth initiatives a disciple builder can employ to stimulate growth. This effective approach accurately represents a biblical model for growth to maturity. Scripture reveals only the broad strokes of this pattern, so we must look to the Holy Spirit to fill in the details. Still, this model holds true to the affirmations of Scripture.

A copy of the R-CAPS Grid is included in Section C of The

Appendix. (You may choose to refer to this as we explain it.) Along the top are the Roman Numerals I-V, which correspond to the phases of spiritual growth: Phase I: Establishing Faith; Phase II: Laying Foundations; Phase III: Equipping for Ministry; Phase IV: Developing New Leaders; Phase V: Developing Mature Leaders. (Some of these phases are broken down into Parts A and B.) Below the Phases are terms which describe people at various levels of spiritual maturity: New Believer, Young Believer, Ministry Trainee, New Leader, and Mature Leader.

Along the left side of the Grid are listed the five growth initiatives, activities which can be used to facilitate growth. These spell out the acronym **R-CAPS**: **R**elationships, **C**ontent, **A**ccountability, **P**rayer, **S**ituations and give the Grid its name.

- R: stands for **Relationships**

- C: for **Content**

- A: for **Accountability**

- P: for **Prayer**

- S: for **Situations**

As you can see, the phases listed across the top (including subdivisions), and the activities listed on the left-hand side of the page produce a grid with forty boxes. Each box contains a word or phrase and a number. The word or phrase describes an objective that relates both to a particular stage of spiritual development and a particular type of activity. The numbers correspond to an accompanying R-CAPS Legend (included in Section C of The Appendix) that gives more detail about that specific objective. (These details are not meant to be exhaustive, but illustrative, showing how tactics change depending on spiritual development.)

The purpose of the Legend is to provide more specific examples for how to relate (R) to the disciple, what content (C) to teach, what traits or activities to hold him accountable (A) for, how to pray (P) for the disciple, and what situations (S) to put him in to encourage growth. Also included in the Legend are a few special notes that elaborate and/or clarify some key points. Please remember this is not a formula but a series of examples of intentional objectives that a disciple builder can plan and implement in the context of a local church. As such, the Grid is a helpful disciple building tool in two ways:

- **Assessment:** A disciple's ability or inability to demonstrate consistency in the objectives listed in the Grid for a specific phase can indicate his position in the growth process to the disciple builder.

- **Planning:** As a disciple builder identifies the disciple's phase of growth and references the growth initiatives (R-CAPS) for that phase, he can better determine appropriate strategies to help the disciple grow.

How a Life Coach Can Use R-CAPS to Design Growth Projects

At some point, most of us have become lost or disoriented in a large suburban mall. Eventually we find the mall guide. A locator map shows the floor plan with an arrow showing our current location along with the location of all the stores. By cross-referencing these pieces of information, we can navigate a path to our destination.

The R-CAPS Grid works in much the same way. It helps us know the floor plan or pattern of spiritual growth. It helps us locate a disciple's position and gives us a set of specific instructions about how to reach the destination or next phase of spiritual growth.

Let's look at an example. A disciple builder must first determine the disciple's location along the phases of growth. To determine this, examine the Accountability row on the R-CAPS Grid (Section C of

The Appendix). The objectives of this row show the disciple's obedience, faith and teachability, which make the best indicators of maturity. WDA also offers the *Christian Growth Checklist,* an even better tool to help you accomplish this task.

Remember: A disciple may appear to be further along than he really is. For example, he may have the knowledge level (Content) or the office (Situation) of a leader but still struggle with issues that reveal his lack of maturity. The wise disciple builder will look at the character and conduct traits indicated in the Accountability row as a more accurate measure of spiritual maturity than Content or Situation.

Let's say you've determined that one of your disciples falls in Phase III, Equipping for Ministry. A primary indicator that he has reached the Ministry Trainee level of maturity is that he has "become ministry-minded" (as we see in the Accountability box #18 on the R-CAPS Grid). Now refer to box #18 of the Legend (in Section C of The Appendix). We observe that he has begun to take responsibility for tasks in the ministry, that he actively takes a stand for the Gospel, and that he has begun to make ministry a priority.

Continuing our example, look at the column under Phase III and locate the objective listed as Mentoring (#16). This is the objective corresponding to the Relationships activity, the "R" in the R-CAPS Grid. This helps you define your role as a disciple builder in the process and the type of relationship most needed to help the disciple grow. More specifically, #16a-c of the Legend tells you that your disciple needs to be a part of a select, but open group; that he needs to meet regularly with a disciple builder who can help him develop specific ministry skills; and that he needs to establish casual, evangelistic relationships with non-Christians.

By referencing the specific activities in each of the other R-CAPS boxes, the disciple builder is able to develop growth projects that will help the disciple move to the next level of maturity. In WDA's *Life*

Coaching Manual, we discuss how to design growth projects for individual disciples. By using a life-planning tool and designing a growth plan (N-G-P) we discover where a disciple is on the journey toward maturity and help him take the next step.

This approach is organized around the concept of discovering individual **needs (N)**, setting specific **goals (G)**, and designing manageable **projects (P)** for spiritual development. By utilizing this tool and following the progressive model outlined in the R-CAPS Grid, a disciple builder is on the way toward helping people grow to maturity in Christ.

But even as we affirm that disciple building can be intentional and practical, following broad patterns of spiritual development arranged around a framework modeled by Christ Himself, we must also remember that the entire process can also be confusing and unpredictable. The wise disciple builder can and should prepare. But part of the preparation involves being ready for unexpected developments, initiatives of a good—but often mysterious—sovereign God. This will require balanced thinking supported by biblical principles and faith.

Employing the five growth initiatives and following a progressive pattern, Jesus laid the foundation for intentional disciple building that would change the world. By studying His ministry approach, we can help modern believers grow to maturity so as to become salt and light in a dark world.

In The Appendix of this book and in other WDA publications, we explain in greater detail how to utilize these five growth initiatives to design overarching programs and individual growth projects that "meet people where they are, and help them take the next step." We are convinced that progressive growth unto maturity can take place in local churches. In fact, that's the way God intended for it to occur.

Thinking Like A Parent

I'll never forget the thrill of bringing our first child home from the hospital. We were so excited about our new baby that I forgot to stop by the nurse's station to pick up the owner's manual. (Later, I discovered there wasn't one.) At the time I reasoned, "How hard can this be? We feed her, clothe her, and love her. So what if she leaks a little at first?"

In spite of my inexperience, everything went fairly well until we reached the twenty-four-month milestone. Then everything changed. Almost overnight, our cute, cuddly toddler turned into a demanding, irascible thug. I soon learned we had entered into a stage of human development not-so-affectionately known as "The Terrible Two's."

Once again, I lamented the absence of the owner's manual. If I'd only known this was going to happen, things could have been drastically different. First, I would have prepared myself emotionally for this little tyrant's arrival. Second, I would have made plans to head off the attempted coup.

Later, I learned to better prepare myself and our children for life's various stages of growth. In fact, I enjoyed learning to understand and then address the ever-changing needs of each child. This requires special wisdom at times, but an understanding of the developmental process provides a definite advantage. Disciple building is a complex process not unlike raising children. Although we can identify patterns of human development, every child is unique.

One of the goals of this book is to provide a simple model that allows the disciple builder to keep overall goals in mind while allowing for individual variations in development. But no manual can substitute for the hard work and devotion that human development requires. Bringing people to maturity is never easy, but it's one of life's most important tasks.

The curriculum and programs mentioned in Section A of The Appendix employ five of the six disciple building situations that provide the context in which growth occurs. The curriculum is designed around community groups, life-coaching (mentor) relationships, the activities of ministry, various instructional formats, and the individual spiritual disciplines. This curriculum intentionally excludes the public gathering of the community of believers, where corporate worship and the preaching of the Word occur as a discipleship environment for the curriculum. But we cannot overstate the impact of pulpit preaching on the developmental process. A faithful, gifted shepherd-teacher is able to convey God's messages for a particular congregation using particular methods in specific, timely ways.

Simple, But Not Simplistic

A friend of mine once remarked, "Golf is a very simple game. All you have to do is knock a ball in a hole with a stick!" Of course, anyone who's ever played golf understands its incredible complexity and the disciplined skill a positive outcome requires.

WDA has painstakingly designed and developed church programs that support and encourage growth to maturity.

Similarly, we believe the R-CAPS process is a useful framework for understanding progressive Christian growth to maturity. However, we don't want to give the impression that disciple building is "simple" in the sense that growth to maturity can be reduced to a one-page matrix. Our overview is beneficial because it provides the architecture for developing a comprehensive, progressive process for growth. Using this grid as a guide, WDA has painstakingly designed and developed church programs that support and encourage growth to maturity.

These programs are supported by a progressive curriculum (including practicum) that integrates theology, emotional (heart) restoration, skills training, and ministry experience. It includes cognitive (head) training, emotional/relational (heart) training, and practical (hands) training and effectively teaches disciples to think, feel, and act like Jesus. Our programs are more than instructive, however. Implemented amid caring relationships that foster appropriate accountability and enhanced by supportive prayer and dependence on God, they work together to produce an environment where faith can thrive.

Some leaders will be able to look at the Grid and use it to design their own creative strategies for growth with resources and structures already in place. WDA enthusiastically encourages this approach and hopes you'll collaborate with us about the tools that have helped you most. Others will need or want more assistance. As mentioned, we offer training seminars, resources, and consultation support to accompany our discipleship programs. Section A of The Appendix contains an overview of The 28/20 Project, which includes an explanation of specific programs that can be implemented in a local church to facilitate growth to maturity.

Jesus' method of disciple building was both relational and dynamic.

We've designed these programs to be more than classes or seminars. They're interactive, focused at various maturation points and carried out in a caring community. Jesus' method of disciple building was both relational and dynamic, carried out in the midst of an active ministry and opposed by human and spiritual forces. He referred to His disciples not only as students, but also as family (Matt. 12:48-49).

All of the R-CAPS disciple building activities and programs should be understood from this perspective. Life situations (S) can put stress on relationships (R), affording opportunities to learn new truths (C) while changing priorities and values (A). Biblical truth (C) often prompts changes in life situations (S) and relationships (R). Relationships (R) can create teaching opportunities (C) and accountability (A) to ensure that the information is put into practice. Changes (S/A/R) move us into and occur because of prayer (P).

The truths Christ taught His disciples unfolded in stages as their understanding increased. Truth builds on itself.

The truths Christ taught His disciples unfolded in stages as their understanding increased. Truth builds on itself. More basic truths lead to an understanding of more complex ones, provided we put our foundation of learning into practice. Internalizing biblical concepts takes time, and, as we have mentioned, some people will need more time than others. Disciple building will never be finished until Christ returns, but we can lay a solid foundation and help people become mature (fully trained, Christlike). The 28/20 Project aims to provide spiritual leaders with a robust, transferable model for spiritual multiplication. WDA is blessed to join you in the journey.

Chapter 6

"When the Chief Shepherd appears..."

Since leaders will give an account to Christ,
we must adopt a philosophy of ministry
that is decidedly biblical.

Being a pastor is a tough job—in my estimation, one of the toughest. For most, the pay is minimal and the hours long and often exhausting. And then there's the spiritual warfare. An effective, faithful pastor walks around with the laser target of a spiritual sniper aimed straight at his heart.

Sometimes the battles are direct, frontal, and emotionally depleting: adrenalin-laced, catastrophic events involving health, finances, and other family matters. But more often, the most difficult battles involve the cold drudgery of discouragement, the enemy's weapon of choice against leaders.

Nehemiah understood discouraging attacks. His opponents

145

sneered, "What are these feeble Jews doing?... Will they finish in a day?... What they are building—even a fox climbing up on it would break their wall of stones!" (Neh. 4:2,3)

What makes these challenges more devastating is the fact that most pastors manage their struggles alone. Few have a faithful group of friends within their congregation who understand and support them emotionally and spiritually. Many feel as if they are dogged by a pack of spiritual hyenas who await every misstep, point out every mistake, and look for every opportunity to criticize. Small wonder that the ministerial fall-out rate is steep and increasing. [31]

The Apostle Paul was a veteran of these wars. At times, his struggles were so intense that he "despaired even of life" (2 Cor. 1:8, NASB). We don't often associate crippling depression with the victorious Christian life, but ministry is full of struggles that, left untended, can progress into clinical concerns. That's why Paul continually urged those in leadership to maintain perspective, setting the difficulties of following Christ against the rewards of eternity: "For our light and momentary troubles are achieving for us an eternal glory that far outweighs them all" (2 Cor. 4:17).

Paul also knew the value of team and encouragement.

Paul also knew the value of team and encouragement. In an astonishing passage in 2 Corinthians 2:12-13, he recognizes an open door for ministry but declines to walk through it until Titus can accompany him.

The apostle Peter also knew spiritual attack and the value of maintaining biblical balance and perspective. He reminded the leaders under his care that, "These (struggles) have come so that the proven genuineness of your faith—of greater worth than gold, which perishes even though refined by fire—may result in praise, glory, and honor when Jesus Christ is revealed" (1 Pet. 1:7).

Peter learned this truth in the throes of battle. The Lord warned him that pride and misplaced priorities had created a situation where the enemy had "demanded permission to sift you like wheat" (Luke 22:31, NASB). And Peter *was* crushed, as his bitter lament after denying Christ reveals. In due course, the Lord reinstated him to ministry (John 21 records the joyful reunion), but the restoration was bittersweet. Christ's three questions reminded Peter of his boasting that he loved the Lord and would never forsake Him, only to deny knowing Him three times during the night of His betrayal. But Peter was also encouraged to realize that his failure had not disqualified him from ministry. The Lord recommissioned Peter three times to look after His flock.

The priority of Peter's renewed calling rang clear: Jesus saw caring for God's sheep as a profound display of love central to His Great Commission. Perhaps Peter also recalled the Ezekiel 34 warning to the selfish shepherds of Israel mentioned earlier. In this passage, God reveals His immense displeasure for the unwillingness of His appointed shepherds to care for His people.

We must stay focused on what the Lord states as His clear priority: caring for His sheep.

Did Jesus have this in mind when He challenged Peter to "Feed my sheep" (John 21:17)? Perhaps so. Christ's claim to be the Good Shepherd is a fulfillment of the Ezekiel prophecy. And if so, the message is a double admonition for those of us who tend sheep in the modern church. We must stay focused on what the Lord states as His clear priority: caring for His sheep.

In his first epistle, Peter continues this emphasis by saying, "Therefore, I exhort the elders among you, as your fellow elder and witness of the sufferings of Christ, and a partaker also of the glory that is to be revealed, *shepherd the flock of God among you, exercising oversight not under compulsion*, but voluntarily, according to the will of God; and not for sordid gain, but with eagerness; nor yet as lording it over those allotted to your charge, but proving to be examples to the flock. And when the Chief Shepherd appears, you will receive the unfading crown of glory" (1 Pet. 5:1-4, emphasis added).

Did you get that? *"When the Chief Shepherd appears..."*

Those who build disciples, caring for the flock of God, must keep our focus on The Day when the Chief Shepherd appears: The Day of The Lord. That's when we'll receive the full reward for our service on earth. In the meantime, we must serve not for selfish gain, or with political motive, or in order to leverage our authority and gain control. We must serve willingly and, if necessary, sacrificially. The crown of glory is worth the investment.

A Lesson from Demas

But compromise becomes easy if we lose perspective. And unfortunately, some shepherds aren't willing to wait. They want immediate benefits and instant glory.

Demas was one such worker. In his second letter to Timothy, Paul urges his young protégé to maintain the same eternal perspective we've discussed: "In the presence of God and of Christ Jesus, who will judge the living and the dead, and in view of his appearing and his kingdom..." (2 Tim. 4:1). He goes on to urge Timothy to be faithful in dispatching his duties as a Christian leader, a builder of disciples who helps God's people grow to maturity.

But he also draws Timothy's attention to those who lose perspective, forsaking and compromising their calling, "Do your best to come to me quickly, for Demas, *because he loved this world* (emphasis added), has deserted me..." (2 Tim. 4:9-10). The details are sketchy, but it appears that Demas didn't leave the ministry altogether. Instead, he went to Thessalonica, a locale other than where he was supposed to be. No disreputable spot, this city was home to a solid work. But as Paul points out, Demas went there in disobedience to the will of God. He left a place that required hardship and sacrifice for a more appealing one.

Unfortunately, many modern shepherds have followed the pattern of Demas. These shepherds care little for building disciples, setting captives free, confronting enemies, caring for the hurting, or watching out for spiritual lambs. Their ministry is more about themselves and their agenda than the flock (the agenda of Jesus). Their priority is often a bigger pulpit or more money. They measure success in numbers of congregants or size of buildings and budgets instead of the markers of maturity Jesus set forth. But sometimes the force that drives their ministry is a desire to control others. Many small churches are led by spiritual bullies who command their congregations through fear and manipulation.

Of course, nothing is inherently wrong with numbers, buildings, or programs. Each can serve as evidence of spiritual effectiveness and of people growing to maturity. Mature people will indeed give more, participate more, serve more sacrificially, lead more effectively, and so on. But these external measurements resemble the number of hits in a baseball game or first downs in a football game. Sports statistics, although worth recording, have a close link to game-winning effectiveness. But they don't measure true success.

In the same way, Christlikeness (not mere program participation) is the outcome for which we must aim, and this requires the often thankless task of tending sheep and feeding lambs. These efforts demand leaders who lay down lives and prerogatives to serve a King who laid down His life for us. Since He may not appear during our lifetime, our service requires faith. But this invitation and warning comes from Jesus Himself.

Jesus urged his leaders to be fearless in the face of persecution but cautious about the world's influence. He warned them to remain on guard against the influence of religious leaders who cared more for their reputations and careers than the Kingdom. Jesus compared the dangerous influence of such false shepherds to yeast that leavens a lump of dough, slight in appearance but powerful in effect. The Pharisees had earned widespread respect. But Jesus labeled them "blind guides" headed for a harsh judgment.

To avoid falling into the Pharisees' trap, we must carefully evaluate our approach to ministry. Both lay leaders and vocational staff must resist the temptation to use worldly models to determine ministry success. We must allow the Scriptures and our Lord to set the bar and define the terms.

Can we learn from both Demas and the Pharisees? Yes, if we agree to soul-searching and an honest appraisal of our hearts and ministry agendas, remembering that, "We must all appear before the judgment seat of Christ" (2 Cor. 5:10). Because of this, we can do nothing less than ask Him to "Search me, God, and know my heart; test me, and know my anxious thoughts. See if there is any offensive way in me, and lead me in the way everlasting" (Ps. 139:23-24).

We can't achieve this alone. Indwelling sin makes us too quick to justify ourselves and too short-sighted to see our own inconsistencies. Effective leadership requires a band of faithful, courageous friends who will be painfully honest, "spurring [us] on to love and good deeds" (Heb. 10:24). But in the current climate of immaturity, wise traveling companions are harder and harder to find.

One of the greatest benefits of reinstating a maturation process in local churches is that, eventually, mature leaders will emerge. They will in turn support existing leaders and serve as catalysts for further leadership development. Avoiding the pitfalls of worldliness requires leaders to demonstrate wisdom, humility, and faith, but the outcome is worth the effort.

Avoiding the pitfalls of worldliness requires leaders to demonstrate wisdom, humility, and faith, but the outcome is worth the effort.

I'm convinced that most Christians want to be mature and faithful. They long to live as courageous promise-keepers who lay down their lives for their families and friends, who are good citizens and productive workers. They want to be free from crippling sin-strategies. They want a deeper, more personal walk with God, experiencing His presence and fullness. The problem does not lie in the motivation but in the process—or lack of it.

It's not too late to address and correct the crisis of maturity in our culture and in the church. But to do so, we must be strategic and decisive in our thinking, holding tight to a process that builds disciples to maturity. Now and in times to come, maturity matters.

Where Do We Go From Here?

As we've seen, maturity matters for many reasons. God has designed us to grow, and our family of origin and the local church make ideal environments for this development. But many families are dysfunctional, and some churches have forgotten how to help their parishioners grow or have neglected the process altogether. As a result, individual believers struggle to mature and Western civilization is in steep moral decline.

But it doesn't have to be this way. The solution, far from simple, will require diligence to implement. Maturity occurs over time, not overnight. We must act swiftly, decisively, and wisely.

Maturity means becoming increasingly conformed to the likeness of Jesus Christ so that we think, feel, and act like Him. We've considered a biblical strategy for helping Christians grow to maturity. It's a progressive process that helps people obey the truths of Scripture and increase their understanding of God and His Kingdom. As believers mature, they gradually change their conduct, belief systems, worldview, and ultimately, their character. Maturity also produces an increased capacity for deepening our relationship with God and others. The ultimate characteristic of maturity is sacrificial love (*agape*).

Jesus had a plan for helping His disciples grow to maturity. The process of disciple building is central to the Great Commission entrusted to the Church and should thus be a priority for Christian leaders. The modern Church needs to rethink how we will accomplish this task. We can look to our Lord's pattern of building disciples. For ease of understanding and use, we can compress His approach into a framework, but we must balance all the dynamics that affect progressive growth.

WDA has developed a set of disciple building programs (The 28/20 Project, Section A of The Appendix) supported by a progressive curriculum that guides local church leaders as they help others grow progressively. For more information about these resources, visit www.disciplebuilding.org and download samples, order resources, or learn more about the process. I would also like to encourage you to become part of an ongoing conversation among other leaders who are striving to implement processes that produce maturity. For more information about joining this conversation, contact: maturitymatters@disciplebuilding.org.

Blessings!

"To Him who is able to keep you from falling and to present you before His glorious presence without fault and with great joy—to the only God our Savior be glory, majesty, power and authority, through Jesus Christ our Lord, before all ages, now and forevermore! Amen" (Jude 24-26).

About The Appendix

The Appendix offers additional resources to help disciple builders better understand and implement progressive growth to maturity. Be aware that The Appendix sometimes has the feel of an operators' manual. As such, it contains assembly guides and some of the detailed principles required to support a complex application process.

(I don't know about you, but I hate operators' manuals! They often contain boring stuff, and I don't like having to read instructions. Like a lot of other guys, I think I should be able to intuitively assemble and operate anything from a space heater to The Space Shuttle.)

So here's my advice: Don't read The Appendix until you're ready to grapple with the assembly process. It's for those who want more nuts and bolts so they can get started.

- **Section A,** *The 28/20® Project,* outlines six flexible and workable programs for launching and sustaining progressive discipleship within a local church. When offered together, the programs form a matrix for helping church members grow to maturity. WDA training consultants can help you discern the order of implementation. It's an approach that addresses the unique needs of your church and adapts to the culture.

- **Section B,** *What Jesus Did/What We Can Do,* provides a side-by-side comparison of how Jesus equipped disciples and how we can implement His approach in a modern setting. It provides a perspective that gives disciple builders encouragement that what Jesus did, we also can do.

- **Section C,** *The R-CAPS Grid and Legend,* further clarifies and amplifies the philosophy of ministry outlined in Chapter 3. A grid-model integrates stages of progressive growth with the growth initiatives mentioned in Chapter 5. Using a numbered reference system, it provides observations that will help the disciple builder understand the needs of a disciple at various stages of growth while offering guidelines for how to meet these needs.

Thanks for reading this far. I hope you will read on. I also encourage you to discuss these matters with your church leadership team in hopes that it stimulates immediate collaboration among those who are building disciples or have a desire to do so.

May God richly bless you as you continue to strive to obey Him, teaching His followers to put everything He commanded into practice, for the glory of His Name!

The 28/20® Project

Disciple Building Programs for a Local Church

Overview of The 28/20® Project

The 28/20 Project (its title comes from Matthew 28:20, "teaching them to obey everything I have commanded you") is a set of local church programs that, with the Spirit's help, enables leaders to present people mature in Christ. The programs consist of written materials, live and online seminars, and consultations that provide an applicable, progressive equipping process of everything Jesus commanded. The project is undergirded by prayer and supported by the strategic relationships, content, and ministry experiences needed to facilitate the development of maturity.

History of The 28/20® Project

For decades, WDA worked primarily with students on college

campuses, and we're proud of this legacy. Our alumni serve as lay and vocational leaders in churches and church agencies around the world.

But a few years ago, the Spirit began to refocus and reshape our ministry profile. An informal survey revealed that, although most of our graduates led mature lives of devotion to Christ and His Kingdom, few seemed able to transfer the campus models of leadership development into their local churches.

The problem stemmed not from a lack of commitment but a lack of an appreciation of the differences between a campus ministry and that of the local church. These realizations caused us to revisit our methodology for achieving our mission of delivering leadership development to the Church worldwide.

We remained convinced that the approach used by Jesus in equipping The Twelve for church leadership could apply to the modern church. Our challenge was to discover how to implement it in our modern context.

First, we tried to design a spiritual formations architecture that captured the philosophy and practices of Christ's methodology but could be implemented in contemporary churches in various cultures. After much prayer, deliberation, and extensive research, the R-CAPS Grid (consisting of both content and practicums) emerged as a framework for designing a progressive disciple building curriculum.

Using this grid as the design architecture, we fashioned a Master Concept Map that captured and sorted all the leadership initiatives, biblical principles, skill sets, theology, and ministry structures Jesus employed. We took time to collect from both Testaments any related concepts that enhanced the material taught by Christ, taking special note of any new or amplified material revealed after the Holy Spirit's coming.

From this Master Map, we developed Amplified Outlines for each of the progressive stages of training derived from our study of the Harmony of the Gospels. We noticed that Jesus repeated many of the themes but also saw a deepening progression of explanations and applications corresponding to the gradual development of His leaders. We realized that as His disciples followed and obeyed Him, He was able to lead them into deeper stages of maturity.

Scripture affirms that the same process applies to today's disciples. Putting truth into practice enhances their capacity to understand more complex concepts (Heb. 5:14-6:1; 1 Cor. 2:6).

From each of the Amplified Outlines, our curriculum team developed Teaching Outlines for every communicable concept, cross-referencing these with other portions of Scripture. These Teaching Outlines became the basic building blocks for our entire curriculum and constitute the core of The 28/20 Project. From these outlines, we developed hundreds of Pocket Principles, guided discussions, leadership manuals, and more. We constantly improve and enhance these resources to reflect, as accurately as possible, "everything [Jesus has] commanded you" (Matt. 28:20).

Despite intense spiritual warfare, we sensed the Lord's leading through every step of this development process. We experienced a significant breakthrough in our curriculum development but also realized that resource materials alone did not meet our clients' needs.

People grow best in action-oriented environments. Without supportive programs, study is important but incomplete. Preaching and teaching alone are insufficient to present people mature in Christ. We must train disciples in the context of ministry, interaction, and faith-building situations. Therefore, using the curriculum we developed, we also designed, field-tested, and refined programs for implementation in local churches. We developed them for use in existing church structures, eliminating the need to build parallel ministries that consumed resources of time, manpower, and finances.

We refined the programs in partnerships with traditional churches who embraced a disciple building ministry philosophy that resulted in the outcome of Christlike maturity. Through a series of providential events, we entered into ministry agreements that have proven beneficial in the design, development and deployment of The 28/20 Project. The leaders of these churches have become trusted friends, valuable collaborators, committed colleagues, and loyal ambassadors of progressive disciple building. Working alongside these leaders, we identified a set of Core Competencies church leaders needed to have in order to help their parishioners grow to maturity. The programs of The 28/20 Project were designed with these competencies in mind.

We're continuing research and development of The 28/20 Project at these churches in hopes of establishing and strengthening them as Training Centers. We hope other churches will benefit from the experience and wisdom already gained. One in particular has emerged as a flagship for progressive disciple building that produces mature leaders and reaches out to other churches around the world. The programs listed below were forged in the crucible of these partnerships, and we're deeply indebted to and grateful for these friends.

For more information on The 28/20 Project, visit us at www.disciplesbuilding.org.

The Six Primary Programs of The 28/20® Project

The purpose of this section is to provide an overview of six primary programs needed to establish The 28/20 Project in an existing local church and to help leaders understand the importance of managing change. Implementing The 28/20 Project using WDA's R-CAPS philosophy, training, and resources will take time. In churches where traditions and ministry approaches are deeply entrenched, it will also require a substantial change of culture. Depth of conviction can help accelerate the pace of change, but people still need time to learn and adapt. A planned transition process helps minimize confusion. We've designed the 28/20 programs to facilitate gradual change without sacrificing transformational growth.

Again, the goal of discipleship goes beyond the communication of content, no matter how biblical that content may be. The ultimate goal is transformational change evidenced by a lifestyle of Christlikeness: increasing obedience, deepening intimacy with God and His people, and an unswerving loyalty to the values and practices of the Kingdom. Fully-committed followers of Christ will look like and act like Him, laying down their lives while championing brotherly love and justice. Processes that produce this type of change and work in local churches will require changing both traditions and cultural dynamics.

Since culture change requires time and wisdom, we recommend a prayerful but timely launch to the Project, implemented patiently and methodically. At first, not everyone needs to participate. The initial goal is to establish a base of committed, experienced leaders amid growing ranks of disciples. As the leadership base grows, the rate of change can increase. The "Launching Approaches" section contains suggested options for launching and expanding The 28/20 Project.

Our experience confirms that a wise launch begins with leadership equipping programs for a select group of more mature Christians and foundational programs for all new Christians. Over time, this approach of building the bridge from both banks will produce better results than instituting sweeping change in several areas at once. Recruiting, orienting, and equipping leaders is more important than fanfare. After critical program components and key leaders are in place, church leaders can share the overarching plan.

When The 28/20 Project is fully developed, it should include all the programs outlined in this section. But they should only be implemented as God provides the leadership and grace to do so. Leaders should be prepared for the opposition and confusion that accompany spiritual warfare. Prayer to bind the strong man (Mark 3:27) and protect program personnel should be an essential part of this process.

Although we envision other programs that help support progressive growth, the following are the six we see as essential during the initial stages:

#1-Design-Build Team

Overview

Specialized leadership training that consists of the overarching philosophical orientation, structural architecture, oversight development, assessment and management skills, cultural change dynamics, and spiritual warfare tactics and strategies.

Deliverable Formats

- Seminar

- Field Ops Manual

- Ongoing Consulting

Elements

- Philosophy of Ministry: R-CAPS

- Ministry Architecture

- Managing Culture Change: Principles and Practices

- Benefits and Costs

- Skills Training

Benefits

- Helps prevent confusion and misunderstanding.

- Helps determine and clarify philosophical alignment.

- Helps recruit leaders.

- Provides oversight and spiritual protection.

The implementation of The 28/20 Project will be unique for every church. Launching and sustaining it will require wisdom and maturity. The Design-Build Team provides the overarching leadership needed to steer the process and move it forward. This team supervises and directs the entire progressive discipleship process. It also integrates and coordinates the various disciple building functions and activities needed to accomplish the mission and outcomes.

Team members work with WDA consultants to provide training and prayer support for Life Coaches, Discipleship Community leaders, and Restoring Your Heart leaders as they design and coordinate their various discipleship projects. This team also oversees the Leadership Institute and supports its faculty. Team members should be skilled in spiritual warfare, able to bind the enemy and provide spiritual protection for the entire process, supporting and encouraging one another. (Design-Build Team members will come under severe attack and later emerge as stronger spiritual warriors and more effective leaders.)

If possible, the team should consist of representative leaders from various strategic ministry groups involved in the discipleship process (e.g. executive staff, community group leaders, ministry leaders, counselors, men's/women's ministry heads, community action group leaders, etc.). Members are selected for multi-year terms to insure continuity and philosophical integrity.

The WDA disciple building process is not a one-size-fits-all program, but a flexible, dynamic structure that should be adapted to fit the specific spiritual anatomy of each church. The Design-Build Team approach allows for God's unique leadership gifting and calling and allows the members to grow as they work together. These dual outcomes offer incalculable value for current leadership and future generations. Careful, patient, and prayerful selection, training, and equipping of this team are essential for the success of all the other programs.

Since the Design-Build Team has the responsibility and task of deciding on the specific applications of all the disciple building programs offered, it should be one of the first discipleship programs established. Ideally, this team should be selected, oriented, and commissioned before publicly launching The 28/20 Project.

#2- Restoring Your Heart

Overview

Training for lay people in leading specialized, safe small groups that encourage relational, emotional, and spiritual health by enabling disciples to identify and remove the hindrances to growth to maturity and complete the developmental tasks that support ongoing growth.

Deliverable Formats

- Resources for One Group (Processing Pain)

- Seminar (live and online)

- Field Ops Manual

- Leadership Manual

- Ongoing Consultation

Elements

- Processing Pain

- Understanding Emotions

- Conquering Shame

- Leaders' Training

- Group Dynamics

Benefits

- Provides healing and restorative functions and applications.

- Creates healthy group dynamics and environments with carry-over application for other groups.

- Allows new leaders to emerge.

- Equips all participants with valuable group skills.

- Helps establish the critical link between pain and spiritual growth.

- Encourages transparency and humility.

- Creates an environment of grace and burden-bearing.

- Forms a seedbed for evangelism.

- Helps demolish strongholds.

- If necessary, opens doors for demonic deliverance.

Restoring Your Heart helps disciples recognize and address the emotional and relational stumbling blocks that might hinder healthy spiritual development (Heb. 12:1-2). Often, our areas of unresolved pain create an environment for indwelling sin to erect strongholds in opposition to the sanctifying work of the Holy Spirit. Recognizing and addressing these points of pain and the resultant lies that cripple growth are essential elements of the discipleship process. The Restoring Your Heart ministry is led by a team that offers training and support through small groups and supported by resources that include directed seminars, web training, and printable materials.

Restoring Your Heart is designed to work in concert with the other 28/20 discipleship structures and programs, but when necessary, it can also operate effectively as a stand-alone project. This can serve as a means of meeting a felt need (emotional restoration) in order to create a deeper appreciation of an often unfelt need, intentional discipleship.

Leaders should understand that this process is coordinated by lay people and does not offset the potential need for professional counseling. Ideally, it should be implemented in close coordination with the opportunity for clinical care. Once The 28/20 Project begins, the Design-Build Team should supervise the implementation of Restoring Your Heart.

One of the important by-products of Restoring Your Heart is the building of the concept of safe community, which acts as spiritual leaven. It will gradually influence all the other environments, helping ensure a grace-oriented atmosphere, necessary for evangelism and spiritual growth.

Another benefit lies in its reinforcement of the need for ongoing repentance. As group members face the pain of their past, they realize the need to bring faulty thinking and disobedient choices under the Lordship of Christ. The Gospel continues to impact the life of a disciple throughout life, bearing fruit long after the initial decision to follow Christ.

#3- Cornerstone
(Phases I and II)

Overview
A curriculum (designed for both individuals and small groups) that helps new believers become grounded in the faith and lays the necessary foundations for ongoing growth to maturity.

Deliverable Formats

- Leader's Guide

- Guided Discussion Booklets

- Opportunity for consultation (if needed)

Elements

- Getting Started (Phase I)

- Knowing God (Phase II)

- Understanding People (Phase II)

- Growing Spiritually (Phase II)

- Bible Readings for Devotional Use

Benefits

- Provides a basis for ongoing, future growth in new Christians.

- Reinforces growth and fosters renewal in more mature Christians.

- Helps equip future leaders.

- Strengthens the assimilation dynamic and process.

- Enhances evangelism and outreach.

Cornerstone provides the critical growth components and structures necessary for a recent convert or a new/young believer to become well-established in his faith and assimilated into the fellowship of the church. The program is designed, resourced, and implemented through a training approach that integrates the proclamation of the

Gospel (evangelism) with effective follow-up. It then provides initial spiritual formation concepts within a rich fellowship so that a new and/or young believer is equipped to follow Christ and become an integral part of church life. Cornerstone is best conveyed via micro-groups (quads or triads) led by Life Coaches but woven into the fabric of the larger discipleship community.

Cornerstone also provides more mature Christians with an opportunity to strengthen and stabilize their faith by revisiting the basic doctrines and experiences of the Christian life. This program can work either in concert with or as an extension of a church's existing small groups and mentoring ministries. The curriculum centers on concepts needed to stabilize and encourage a new Christian, followed by a triad of foundational principles: Knowing God, Understanding People, and Growing Spiritually.

The Cornerstone curriculum is designed to run for approximately one year. Once established, it runs continuously with various entry points. Ideally, it should work in concert with the corps of Life Coaches, who meet with and help orient disciples to the Christian life and the church community, facilitating and supplementing their involvement in a Discipleship Community. WDA recommends that each church integrate its own New Members Orientation into the program as well.

#4- Life Coaching

Overview

Training for lay leaders who aspire to "meet people where they are and help them take the next step" of growth to maturity. Offers a philosophical approach and is carried out through the design and implementation of practical growth projects tailored to individual needs and levels of maturity. Church Goal: a Coaching Corps (with various functions and applications).

Deliverable Formats

- Seminar

- Field Ops Manual

- Workshops

- Ongoing Consultation

Elements

- Philosophy and Approach

- Project Design and Implementation (NGP)

- Case Studies

- Organizational Design

- Target Training for Specialties

- Job Descriptions

- Process Page/Flow Chart

Benefits

- Recruits and mobilizes new/potential leaders.

- Develops new leaders.

- Strategically leverages natural and spiritual gifts.

- Provides a prudent organization of labor.

- Allows for incremental expansion.

- Reinforces maturity as an outcome.

- Provides support for all existing ministries.

Life Coaching is designed to train specific spiritual leaders (coaches) how to "meet people where they are and help them take the next step" in their spiritual development. An ideal growth situation occurs when Life Coaches are both embedded in Discipleship Communities to help group members implement teaching and scattered throughout various church ministries to support implementation. This program is especially beneficial for men's and women's ministries, helping equip Leadership Teams (deacons, elders, etc.), or in concert with the Children-Youth Ministry or Next Generation Ministry. Life Coach training can equip anyone who wants more help in working with others one on one, which makes it beneficial for the workplace, in school settings, and in the home.

The training is delivered through a series of workshops and training classes offered periodically that present WDA's NGP skill set, use of a spiritual assessment tool(s), and supportive growth concepts. Other skill sets and concepts can be added as needed or desired. The ultimate objective is a Life Coaching Corps/Fellowship that meets regularly for encouragement and ongoing equipping.

#5- Leadership Development
(Phases III – V)

Overview

A comprehensive curriculum for equipping leaders through five successive levels of development. Covers theological concepts, ministry skills, and practical methods. Though focused on a lay audience, the program is beneficial for those evaluating or entering vocational ministry.

Deliverable Formats

- Teaching Outlines/Guided Discussions/Pocket Principles

- Skills Training Manuals (various)

- Discipleship Community Coordination Guide

- Interactive Group Sessions

Elements

- Leadership 101: Equipping Potential Leaders
  (Resource-Equipping for Ministry-WDA Phase III)

- Leadership 201: Equipping New Leaders, Part 1
  (Resource-Developing New Leaders-WDA Phase IV-A)

- Leadership 301: Equipping New Leaders, Part 2
  (Resource-Developing New Leaders-WDA Phase IV-B)

- Leadership 401: Equipping Established Leaders, Part 1
  (Resource-Developing Mature Leaders-WDA Phase V-A)

- Leadership 501: Equipping Established Leaders, Part 2
  (Resource-Developing Mature Leaders-WDA Phase V-B)

Benefits

- Equips and develops mature leaders.

- Links leadership experience and training.

- Leverages Discipleship Community experiences.

- Fosters unity and peace.

- Solidifies congregational stability.

- Supports and reinforces executive leadership.

- Multiplies overall ministry impact.

- Allows for expansion.

Like any organization, the church needs leaders to develop and accomplish mission objectives. Disciple building churches require leaders who are conformed to the likeness of Christ and skilled in ministry implementation. The Leadership Institute prepares church members for works of service and equips them to equip others.

Potential leaders learn, serve, and fellowship together as they focus on becoming fishers of men in the context of special training experiences coordinated with Discipleship Communities. Training consists of weekly meetings for prayer, team-building, ministry co-ordination, skill-development, and theological study. Participation in the Institute is by invitation only, reserved for Christians who have been tested and proven faithful. Before long, overseers will emerge who are able to sustain existing programs and expand to new fields of service.

The training, delivered by experienced faculty, is organized around modular courses that focus on critical theological growth con-cepts and ministry skills. Practicums are supervised and imple-mented by Life Coaches, who oversee field experiences within Discipleship Communities and alongside standing ministries. Appro-priate challenges facilitate faith development while providing lead-ership and manpower for ministry growth.

Leadership Development helps people find their ministry niche as they learn important concepts in preparation for present and future leadership roles. The goal is to encourage people to become servant leaders, fully equipped to love Christ and His people sacrificially. The length of the process will vary depending on the pace of training and church demographics. As leaders gain experience and deepen their maturity, they ascend to positions of greater responsibility (Luke 16:10). The training, delivered in a team setting using classroom in-struction, group dynamics, and field experiences, consists of five pro-gressive platforms.

#6- Discipleship Communities

Overview

The architecture and operational tactics for launching and sustaining a mid-size (fifteen to forty people), open (various stages of growth) group, consisting of various sub-groups, that can create a movement and thus establish the ideal environment for progressive growth.

Deliverable Formats

- Seminar

- Field Ops Manual

- Ongoing Consulting

Elements

- Architecture

- Philosophy / Approach

- Group Dynamics

- Model Schedule

- Practical How-to's

- Life Coach deployment and coordination

Benefits

- Provides backdrop and setting for Leadership Development.

- Creates genuine community.

- Facilitates evangelism.

- Encourages numerical growth.

Earlier, we mentioned the challenges of transferring a campus paradigm into a local church. But the structure of Discipleship Communities serves both environments well. Most effective campus ministries are built around a group on mission. As Christian students connect with their peers, an ideal growth environment is created for both believers and outsiders. Discipleship Communities constitute a primary structure for such growth (The "S" of the R-CAPS architecture). Although classroom instruction and one-to-one coaching are beneficial and valuable, without a community-context oriented around ministry, concept training will not produce the desired outcome of maturity.

As leaders understand the advantages and dynamics of this format, they can make more informed decisions about the best approach for their congregation. Due to traditional small group structures, establishing this program often requires wisdom and strategic planning. Some churches employ a traditional Sunday School or Bible study paradigm. Others utilize cell groups that meet on site, in homes, or elsewhere. Modifying existing small groups into Discipleship Community structures will require patience and strategic instruction, but the benefits will offset the effort.

Not all existing small groups will make a smooth transition. Some should remain in place rather than be transformed into Discipleship Communities. In some cases, the best approach is not to expect long-standing groups to change without significant acceptance among members. Our experience has taught us that Discipleship Communities are often best constructed with younger believers, led by members of the Discipleship Team.

The emergence of the Missional Community movement, similar in concept and design to Discipleship Communities, has helped many churches understand and embrace the strategic nature of this paradigm. Discipleship Communities play a critical role in providing the environment for progressive spiritual growth, especially in the area of leadership development. Several design parameters set discipleship communities apart from other, more common small group structures.

Discipleship Community Design Parameters

- Ideal size: 15-40 members.

- Has a progressive discipleship function and intention.

- Has a specific mission.

- An open group (actively looking for new members).

- A target audience and focused approach to ministry.

- Can be strategically connected to a larger congregation.

- Contains multiple structures and meeting times based on function.

- Can be subdivided into smaller groups of three to four for mutual accountability, application of truth, and progressive equipping.

- Contains tiered/progressive phases of spiritual growth:

  - Interested contacts

  - New/young believers

  - Potential leaders

  - Developing leaders

  - Established leaders

- Led by a team with multiple gifts/callings/responsibilities.

- Contains embedded Life Coaches who are able to design and implement specific growth projects for members.

28/20® Launching Approaches

Since every church is unique, the launching of The 28/20 Project should be crafted to fit its culture, leadership availability, current commitments, resources, and existing structures. Changes will almost certainly need to occur, but a practical, incremental implementation process will help ensure success.

The most important first step is to orient and unify the existing leadership core. WDA provides orientation experiences and resources to help churches manage the launch. This includes an evaluation of the existing culture, consideration of available resources (manpower, time, and finances), and a consultation to determine the best approach.

Possible launching approaches:

- Equip the Design-Build Team.

- Offer Cornerstone to all current members.

- Implement Restoring Your Heart.

- Train a contingent of Life Coaches.

Conclusion

Many valuable resources are available in the discipleship marketplace to help people grow to maturity. WDA is proud to be part of several networks made up of organizations committed to this outcome and are grateful for the wisdom and understanding God has given in recent years.

Our experience has taught us much about helping local churches implement progressive discipleship programs that can be implemented without undue stress on existing programs and structures. But we don't want to leave anyone with the impression that we have it all figured out. We're committed to ongoing research, discovery, and development. We believe a progressive approach will produce the desired outcome of Christlike maturity and are equally convinced that local churches will be able to apply the programs we mention.

WDA currently delivers training resources to support the six programs using three platforms:

- **Printed/printable materials**: These consist of books, pocket principles, workbooks, guided discussions, teaching outlines, operations manuals, leader's manuals, etc. They equip leaders to help others mature. These resources are either printed, print-ready, or available as e-products, and some are available in a variety of languages for international use.

  Our policy is never to allow price to deter those who are sincere in their desire to use our resources. Others have invested so these materials can be available at a reduced cost or, in some cases, free. If you're able to pay, we hope you'll recognize the value and, if possible, include a donation to supplement costs for those who can't afford them. (For more information on our distribution prices and procedures, see our website.)

- **Seminars**: We offer conferences (live and DVD) and webinars that provide content and interaction around a particular theme or series.

- **Consultation**: Sometimes leaders need to ask questions and interact with other leaders. This can occur online, via teleconference, or in person.

For more information about how this training might fit your situation, contact us at **maturitymatters@disciplebuilding.org.**

As helpful as we've designed these formats to be, spiritual growth is not delivered primarily through curriculum and training. As we've emphasized throughout this book, the best growth occurs in relationship as caring leaders invest their lives in others. We hope the resources God has enabled us to develop will prove beneficial to your church, but your best approach to growth lies in coming alongside others. Let's pray and work together in hope that our combined efforts to fulfill the Great Commission will include teaching disciples to obey everything that Jesus commanded, with true Christlikeness as the outcome.

Maturity matters!

What Jesus Did –
What We Can Do

Phase I: Establishing Faith

Primary Goal: To reach out to unbelievers and proclaim the Gospel in an effort to establish faith in Christ alone for salvation, and conduct basic follow-up with new Christians.

What Jesus Did		What We Can Do
Jesus and John the Baptist: •Went to the lost sheep of Israel and showed concern and care for their spiritual condition by delivering a tough message, laced with love •Gathered people who needed to hear the message and those who had responded to the message *Isaiah 40:3 cf. 42:3/Matthew 9:12 "I have come to call sinners."*	Relationships	•Build relationships with unbelievers in an attempt to "connect"
•Taught God's love, holiness, the atonement of the Lamb of God, the future judgment, the role of the Holy Spirit, evangelistic apologetics, and the divine nature of Christ *John 1:29-34 "Behold the Lamb of God who takes away the sin of the world."*	Content	•Share with unbelievers the Good News and answer their questions about the Christian faith •Follow up with those who respond
•Called people to repent, turn away from contemporary idols and put their trust in God's deliverer (Messiah) •Exhorted the people to become followers (disciples) of this Promised One *Matthew 3:1-2 "Repent, for the Kingdom of Heaven is near."*	Accountability	•Challenge people to repent, accept Christ and publicly declare their faith in Him

What Jesus Did		What We Can Do
•Asked God to call men to become Christ's disciples •Asked that the strong man would be bound and the power of the enemy broken so the Word might be proclaimed Matthew 16:19 "Whatever you bind on earth will be bound in heaven."	**Prayer**	•Pray for opportunities to share Christ with unbelievers •Pray and prepare for the spiritual attacks •Pray that people will become aware of their own emotional needs
•Had various evangelistic encounters and situations where relationships could be established •Had large groups, small groups (in homes and at public gatherings) and individual contacts Matthew 9:10 "While Jesus was having dinner at Matthew's house, many tax collectors and sinners came and ate with Him and His disciples."	**Situations**	•Conduct evangelistic outreaches in communities •Hold evangelistic socials in our homes and churches •Provide opportunities for new disciples to publicly confess their faith in Christ

©WDA 1997-2014

Scriptures from The Harmony of the Gospels:
Matthew 3:1 - 4:11; Mark 1:1-13; Luke 2:1-2, 3:3-18,21-23, 4:1-13; John 1:19-28

Phase II: Laying Foundations

Primary Goal: To gather young believers into a small group to help them understand the foundational truths of the Christian life and involve them in the larger Christian community.

What Jesus Did   What We Can Do

What Jesus Did		What We Can Do
•Challenged a group of disciples to be with Him •Spent time with them individually and as a group •Revealed His identity as Messiah John 1:39 "Rabbi, where are you staying?" "Come and you will see!"	**Relationships**	•Gather an "open" group of young believers who desire to grow •Begin spending time getting to know each of them •Create an honest, safe, grace-oriented, sharing environment that facilitates trust & emotional safety
•Revealed Himself to them as the Messiah through His teaching and miracles •Taught that the Kingdom of God under Messianic rule had appeared and that God had provided an opportunity for them to participate John 2:11 "He thus revealed His glory, and His disciples put their faith in Him."	**Content**	•Teach new disciples the "foundational truths" of the Christian life: The person and work of Christ, the ministry of the Holy Spirit, the sovereign plan of God, and how to grow spiritually
•Challenged them to put their faith fully in Him as their Teacher and Guide •Challenged some to become His followers John 1:43 "Finding Phillip He said to him, 'Follow me.'"	**Accountability**	•Challenge them to be committed to learning how to grow by having a Quiet Time and being around other believers •Invite them to participate in a small group •Encourage them to share emotions & needs •Identify emotional trauma & faulty belief systems •Encourage them to look to God to meet their needs in answer to their specific prayers

What Jesus Did		What We Can Do
• Asked God the Father to call men to follow Him and reveal that He was the Christ •Prayed that power would be made available to accomplish attesting miracles *John 1:47ff. (to Nathaniel) "I saw you when you were under the fig tree...you shall see... angels ascending and descending on the Son of Man."*	**Prayer**	•Ask God to reveal Himself to these new disciples in powerful and intimate ways, answering their prayers and helping them gain insights into His nature and power
•Performed miracles attesting to His divine nature and authority •Set up various teaching situations both publicly and privately •Established His Messianic authority over Israel by cleansing the Temple •Formed a group of followers and took them with Him as He taught and performed miracles *John 3:2 (Nicodemus) "Rabbi, no one could perform the miraculous signs you are doing if God were not with him!"*	**Situations**	•Provide opportunities for new followers to become involved in the Christian community by delegating logistical tasks •Provide social functions to establish relationships with more mature believers •Assign an accountability partner •Be prepared for the Lord to precipitate specific needs that He will provide for

©WDA 1997-2014

Scriptures from The Harmony of the Gospels:
Matthew 4:12-17; Mark 1:14-15; Luke 3:19-20, 4:14-31; John 1:29 - 4:54

Phase III: Equipping for Ministry

Primary Goal: To equip the disciples for ministry in the Kingdom and learn more about the nature of the Kingdom and the principles which govern their role as citizens who are sons and daughters.

What Jesus Did   What We Can Do

What Jesus Did		What We Can Do
•Challenged a few of His disciples to participate in His mission of winning the souls of people •Allowed them to follow Him into spiritual battles and observe His power and authority •Trained them as apprentices working alongside a Master *Mark 1:16ff. "He saw Simon and his brother Andrew casting a net into the sea...and said to them, 'Come, follow Me, and I will send you out to fish for people.'"*	**Relationships**	•Encourage our disciples to be with us as we model a ministry lifestyle •Model healthy relationships •Set & respect boundaries •Be willing to confront others in a caring way •Maintain priorities, and model other aspects of healthy relationships
•Stressed the importance of telling others about His mission and love for sinners •Trained them in basic ministry skills •Gave them insights into the nature of His Kingdom: He was Conqueror over the kingdom of darkness; had authority to forgive sin, heal sickness, and dispel demons *Luke 5:23ff. "Which is easier to say, 'Your sins are forgiven....'?"*	**Content**	•Offer training in evangelism skills •Teach about the sovereign authority of Christ over the spiritual realm and the traditions of men •Review the truths of the Gospel with the purpose of helping others understand •Teach and model healthy relationships •Teach about positional truth
•Called His disciples to be fishers of men •Challenged them to leave their worldly pursuits (at least temporarily) and follow Him on mission *Matthew 4:20 "At once they left their nets and followed Him."*	**Accountability**	•Challenge people to go with us as we reach out to the lost in our community •Challenge them to get training in how to win others to Christ •Encourage them to participate in various ministry situations •Construct projects that address emotional/spiritual strongholds

What Jesus Did   What We Can Do

Prayer

•Prayed for healing power and deliverance for those trapped in sin and satanic strongholds
•Asked for their eyes to be opened to see and understand the spiritual battles raging around them •Prayed for another generation of disciples to repent and follow Him

II Kings 6 (Elisha's servant) cf. Matthew 16:13-19

•Ask God to open doors for our disciples to share their faith •Pray God would give them a vision and burden for the lost •Ask God to free them from emotional and relational bondage

Situations

•Took His disciples on a short-term mission project to upper Galilee •Challenged the status quo of religious traditions and human philosophies •Healed the sick and cast out demons

Matthew 4:23 "Jesus went throughout Galilee, teaching in their Synagogues, preaching the Good News of the Kingdom, and healing every disease and sickness."
John 3:2 (Nicodemus) "Rabbi...no one could perform the miraculous signs you are doing if God were not with him!"

•Take our disciples with us as we minister •Make time to debrief after our ministry times together •Offer opportunities to focus on ministry events, thus showing a willingness to change traditions for the sake of extending the Kingdom (retreats, concerts of prayer, evangelism training, mission projects, restorative opportunities, etc)

Scriptures from The Harmony of the Gospels:
Matthew 4:13-25, 8:2-4,14-17, 9:1-17, 12:1-21; Mark 1:16 - 3:12; Luke 4:31 - 6:11; John 5:1-47

Phase IV: Developing New Leaders

Primary Goal: To appoint a group of leaders and train them to apply kingdom principles as they assist in the ministry and help others grow.

What Jesus Did		What We Can Do
•Appointed the Twelve to be with Him as leaders in His ministry •Allowed them to assume important ministry roles and gave them authority •Sent them out in pairs to preach and minister in His Name •Spent extra time instructing them as a group and individually *Luke 6:13 "He called His disciples to Him and chose twelve of them."*	**Relationships**	•Appoint leaders •Train leaders as they assume roles of responsibility in the overall ministry and over individuals •Be prepared to provide encouraging perspective when God challenges their status quo
•Taught the principles of Kingdom life as being distinct from religious traditions •Explained that true religion was from the heart and not merely external acts •Taught the eternal nature of God's plan and purpose and the wisdom of placing priority on eternal over temporal matters •Taught principles of spiritual authority and warfare *Matthew 5-7 (Sermon on the Mount)*	**Content**	•Teach basic leadership skills •Explain that true discipleship will produce Christlikeness and that biblical ministry involves growth in character, not just success in ministry programs •Teach about spiritual warfare, problem solving, team dynamics and how to resolve conflict
•Challenged their human propensity to put their trust in themselves and the temporal systems of men •Tested them by disrupting their life and ministry •Jeopardized the success of His public ministry to emphasize the importance of internal obedience, faith, and eternal priorities *John 6:5 "Where shall we buy bread for these people to eat?"*	**Accountability**	•Allow our disciples to fail •Challenge them to assume responsibility in ministry tasks that appear bigger than their abilities •Help them rearrange their priorities around their new responsibilities

What Jesus Did

What We Can Do

Prayer

•Prayed that God would give wisdom in selecting the disciples who were ready for leadership •Asked that they might see the greatness of God and their own insufficiency and that God would provide supernaturally

Luke 6:12 "Jesus went out to a mountainside to pray, and spent the night praying to God. When morning came...."

•Pray for wisdom in the leadership selection process •Ask that they might see the greatness of God and their own insufficiency •Ask God to provide for them supernaturally

Situations

•Gave them real responsibilities in His ministry •Set up ministry situations that required supernatural provision and demanded faith •Created a new structure in His ministry: the Leadership Team which allowed Him opportunities to apply truth at a deeper level by instructing these leaders separately from the main body of disciples and/or the interested others •Required them to spend more time with Him and the work, thus causing them to reevaluate their priorities

John 6 "Do not work for the food which perishes, but...endures."

•Help them develop the gifts God has given them by positioning them in roles that suit them •Send them into situations that will be sure to invite spiritual warfare •Give them responsibilities to disciple and mentor young believers •Include them in the Leadership Team

Scriptures from The Harmony of the Gospels:
Matthew 5:1 - 17:23; Mark 3:13 - 9:32; Luke 6:12 - 9:45; John 6:1 - 7:1

Phase V: Developing Mature Leaders

Primary Goal: To develop a group of mature disciples who have a vision for reaching the nations through God's enabling power, and to have an ability to make other disciples according to the pattern Jesus used.

What Jesus Did		What We Can Do
•Reduced their dependence on him while continuing to have an intimate relationship with them by giving them more independence and slowly weaning them from Himself •Challenged them to be committed to one another •Washed their feet •Laid down His life on the Cross John 15:15-17 "I have called you friends, for everything that I learned from My Father I have made known to you. ...Love each other."	**Relationships**	•Focus our training and attention on our disciples' full development •Commission them as peers in ministry •Continue to serve and love them as friends
•Taught the importance of reaching all the nations, the all-sufficiency of the Spirit, the inadequacy of human strength, the importance of unity in the Body, how the church should function and how to demonstrate agape love in the midst of relational struggles John 17:23 "May they be brought to complete unity to let the world know that you sent me...."	**Content**	•Teach the importance of unity, reaching the nations, suffering love, and (advanced) leadership skills •Teach the dynamics of family life and church life •Remind them that though they have been trained, discipleship is never fully completed until we stand before Christ
•Challenged them to love one another •Commanded them to feed and care for His sheep •Challenged them to go into the entire world and make disciples John 15:17 "This is my command: Love each other."	**Accountability**	•Challenge them to consider what worldwide mission involvement would look like for them •Exhort them to set aside petty differences and strive to put each other first •Suggest they become less dependent on us as mentors and form new ministry relationships

What Jesus Did		What We Can Do
•Prayed they would be able to overcome the enemy and their fleshly self-sufficiency •Asked that they would experience the fullness and enabling of the Holy Spirit Luke 22:31 "Simon, Simon, Satan has asked to sift you like wheat. But I have prayed for you."	**Prayer**	•Pray God would allow them to humbly rest in the power of Christ's Spirit in them •Ask for unity and love to prevail as the enemy puts stress on relationships •Ask God to give them a vision and burden for the entire world
•Gave them increased responsibility in leading the ministry •Moved His ministry beyond the borders of Palestine •Commanded them to go into the entire world to make disciples and then teach these disciples to put into practice the same things they had been taught Matthew 28:18-20 "Go and make disciples of all nations...."	**Situations**	•Include them as part of a leadership team that directs the larger ministry •Take the Great Commission seriously by setting up discipleship training and world missions opportunities •Watch for the Lord to put our disciples, and us, in situations where they/we are incapable of pulling ministry off in our own strength

©WDA 1997-2014

Scriptures from The Harmony of the Gospels:
Matthew 17:24 - 28:20; Mark 9:33 - 16:20; Luke 9:46 - 24:53; John 7:2 - 21:25; Acts 1:1 - 2:4

The R-CAPS Grid and Legend

The R-CAPS Grid:
Strategy for the Disciple Builder

Phases of Christian Growth:

Phase *I*
Establishing Faith

Phase *II*
Laying Foundations

	Part A Cultivating Interest	Part B Providing Follow-up	

	New Believer ▶		**Young Believer** ▶
R *Relationships*	Showing Concern 1	Initiating 6	Nurturing 11
C *Content*	Gospel 2	Follow-up 7	Foundational Truths 12
A *Accountability*	Seeks God, Repents and Believes 3	Begins to Grow 8	Cultivates Relationships with God and Christians 13
P *Prayer*	Salvation 4	Assurance 9	Understanding and Growth 14
S *Situations*	Opportunity to respond to Gospel 5	Opportunity to Break with Old Life 10	Involvement in Body of Christ 15

Phase *III*
Equipping for Ministry

Phase *IV*
Developing New Leaders

Phase *V*
Developing Mature Leaders

	Part A Appointing New Leaders	**Part B** Focusing on Eternal Things	**Part A** Delegating New Respon- sibilities	**Part B** Casting a World Vision

Ministry Trainee ▶ **New Leader** ▶ **Mature Leader**

Mentoring 16	Training 21	Encouraging 26	Delegating 31	Commis- sioning 36
Law and Grace 17	Leadership Principles: Character, Authority 22	Eternal Perspective 27	Team Ministry 32	Resurrection Power in Daily Life 37
Becomes Ministry-Minded 18	Assumes Leadership Responsibili- ties 23	Adjusts Expectations 28	Fosters Unity 33	Shows Sacri- ficial Love to Reach the World 38
Courage/Provision 19	Perspective/ Wisdom 24	Endurance 29	Unity in Diversity 34	Sacrificial Love 39
Opportunity to Serve and Witness 20	Appoint- ment to Leadership Role 25	Acceptance of Difficult Assignments 30	Ability to Work with Other Leaders 35	Acceptance of Worldwide Challenge 40

The R-CAPS Legend
Strategy for the Disciple Builder

Phase I
Establishing Faith

Part A — Cultivating Interest

Showing Concern (R) Disciple Builder:

1a   Goes into unbeliever's world: relates in casual, social situations; develops friendships with those who are open; shows compassion; meets felt needs.

1b   Invites those who are curious to get together in groups.

1c   Is transparent about his beliefs in the normal course of conversation. Doesn't hide who he is, but also doesn't press his views.

Disciple Builder: The goal here is to show unbelievers the love of Christ. You should enter into their world and show love, compassion and genuine interest. Show them in practical ways that the love of Jesus is relevant and sufficient to meet their needs. Also, be available to answer questions.

Gospel (C) Disciple Builder:

2a   Addresses felt needs from a biblical perspective: relationships, self-esteem, career, etc. as a way of showing God's love and holiness.

2b   Answers questions and objections (apologetics).

2c   Presents plan of salvation: e.g., God's justice, wrath, judgment, love, mercy, grace and forgiveness; Christ's substitution; and our need for genuine repentance and faith.

Disciple Builder: It's important to focus on meeting a person's felt needs — areas he wants help in (marriage, parenting, finances, etc.). Address these from a biblical perspective as interest and the relationship allow. That is, if the person is somewhat hostile to spiritual issues, you might not directly refer to what the Bible says about a particular issue. Be sensitive.

When a person is interested in spiritual things, the leader can introduce him to more biblical information. However, it is important that the leader be sure that this biblical information is presented in understandable, relevant terms (not Christian jargon that may be meaningless or overwhelming). The person needs to know the basics of God's character and how to become a Christian. You as the leader need to discern what is holding the person back and plan appropriately. (For example, if it is a heart/willingness issue, you may need to pray and continue being a friend. If there is a specific issue hindering the person, you may need to help resolve that issue.)

Seeks God, Repents and Believes (A) Unbeliever:

3a   Shows interest in knowing more about God (e.g., responds to an invitation to a Christian event).

3b   Begins to think about God and ask questions.

3c   Confesses, repents and puts faith in God (makes restitution, if necessary).

Disciple Builder: To become a believer, the person must repent and make a decision to follow Christ. His life will begin to change, and you will begin to see fruit. Do not rush this transition. Genuine repentance is essential to growth.

Salvation (P) Disciple Builder prays:

4a   For open doors, boldness and words to speak.

4b   For God to break down strongholds and build interest in unbeliever.

4c   For repentance and faith in God (for unbeliever to see sin, believe in God's judgment, understand God's message of repentance, understand and respond to God's love and forgiveness, gain respect for God and His Word, and for God to expose idols in the person's life).

Disciple Builder: Much of the work will be done by the Holy Spirit in the person's heart. Prayer is essential.

Opportunity to Respond to Gospel (S) Disciple Builder:

5a   Puts unbeliever or new Christian in situations in which he can experience God's love and character through Christians. For example: invites unbeliever to evangelistic Bible study (or meets one-to-one to discuss a study); invites to socials, etc. with Christians.

5b   Looks for situations in which disciple builder can help meet the person's needs.

Disciple Builder: Usually you will be with unbelievers or new Christians in daily situations of life (at the gym, dinner after work, a coffee break, a camping trip, etc.), not special religious events. Be sensitive to the person's level of interest and do not push him. Also, ask the person to help you with something (a household repair or another area he has expertise in). This willingness to ask for help demonstrates a humility that is attractive and builds the relationship. As a person becomes interested in spiritual things, you can be more direct by inviting him to Bible studies, etc. Again, however, you need to be careful not to overwhelm him with information or pressure him to make a commitment.

Part B — Providing Follow-Up

Initiating (R) Disciple Builder:

6a   Intentionally initiates with the new believer in order to begin the follow-up process.

6b   Continues to develop a casual friendship with new believer.

Follow-Up (C) Disciple Builder:

7a   Shares basic follow-up information: assurance of salvation, baptism, fellowship with other believers, importance of the Word, basics of prayer and Bible study.

7b   Teaches benefits of following Christ: fellowship in Christ, eternal security in Christ.

Disciple Builder: These are the truths that form the basis of the life and growth of a Christian. The author of Hebrews refers to the "elementary teachings" in Hebrews 6:1. Understanding and beginning to live these truths is essential since Christlikeness is the goal.

Begins to Grow (A) New Believer:

8a   Begins to grow: associates with other Christians, grows in assurance in relationship with Christ, takes steps to learn more.

8b   Begins to practice repentance daily (life begins to change); demonstrates humility.

8c   Publicly identifies with Christ and His body (through baptism).

Disciple Builder: At this point, you will begin to see changes in the new believer's life. It is difficult to list specific changes to look for because they vary based on the person's need and the sovereign choice of God. However, the changes will occur primarily in the areas of attitude toward God and others. Some "sin" areas (especially habits that are deeply ingrained) may remain because the new believer is still quite young in his relationship with God. Be careful not to expect too much too soon or to impose legalistic standards. The person is ready to move on to Phase II: Laying Foundations when he understands and has begun to practice the follow-up truths.

Assurance (P) Disciple Builder prays:

9a   For protection as the Gospel takes hold.

9b   For a teachable heart.

9c   For new believer to be in situations in which he can see God at work in and for him.

9d   For new believer to understand the assurance of his salvation, his eternal security, the fact that God loves him, the forgiveness of his sins, the fact that the Holy Spirit dwells in him, that the Bible is the Word of God.

Disciple Builder: Many ingredients go into the new Christian's growth in his new life in Christ: enjoying fellowship with other Christians, becoming acquainted with the Bible, understanding what God has done in his life, getting to know Jesus, dealing with sin areas in his life, etc. Prayer is essential as the new believer and the disciple builder look to God as the source of growth.

Opportunity to Break with Old Life (S) Disciple Builder:

10a   Invites new believer to attend a small group (or one-to-one appointments) for follow-up study.

10b   Looks for opportunities for the new believer to fellowship with Christians.

10c   Gives new believer the opportunity to confess his new faith in various situations.

Disciple Builder: It should not be expected that the new believer's testimony be smooth or technically perfect at this point in his development. (At Phase III: Equipping for Ministry, time will be spent sharing how to prepare a testimony.) The purpose of giving the new believer opportunities to talk about what God has done in his life (salvation) is to encourage him and solidify the commitment he has made.

Phase II
Laying Foundations

Nurturing (R) Disciple Builder:

11a   Begins leading an open and safe group (i.e., people may come and go) in which relationships can develop (informal; not a long-term personal commitment).

11b   Gives new disciple a chance to grow in love for and commitment to other believers.

11c   Continues to develop a trust relationship with disciple. Begins to model tasks (using the "steps of transfer" listed below) undertaken in the ministry (witnessing, sharing testimony). The relationship is casual, but disciple builder is available.

Disciple Builder: The term "steps of transfer" refers to the procedure used in training a disciple in a skill or activity. The steps of transfer are: Observation (O), Participation (P), Supervision (S), and Independence (I). Note that the abbreviation "OPSI" is used in this Legend. At the step of Observation, a disciple watches as the leader performs a task or activity. At the Participation step, he performs the task or activity with the leader. In the Supervision step, a disciple performs the task or activity alone, but with the supervision of the leader. At the last step of transfer, Independence, a disciple works on his own, independent of the disciple builder.

The commitment referred to in 11a and 11b is not an extensive, formal commitment, but a relational commitment. It is a commitment based on a personal relationship developed with Jesus, with the leader and with others in the small group. The "safe" atmosphere of the small group (mentioned in 11a) comes from the trust relationships built between the disciple and the leader and to a lesser extent between the disciple and other group members. The leader needs to create an atmosphere of grace – an environment in which there is an assurance of receiving love and where confidentiality is maintained so that there can be honesty about struggles and problems. As the leader gets to know the disciple, he will begin to see emotional and relational problems (if any). As trust develops, the leader can begin to gently expose them. If they are severe, he can help the disciple find help.

Foundational Truths (C) Disciple Builder:

12a Teaches about the person and work of Christ: deity, authority, power, sovereignty, Lordship.

12b Shares how to walk daily with Christ: importance of obedience, daily acceptance by grace, role and work of the Holy Spirit, spiritual disciplines, basic principles of divine guidance.

12c Shows in Scripture that Christ is the intercessor and helper for all needs.

12d Shares how to deal with emotions (past and present).

12e Helps disciple develop a better understanding that God created people with needs and emotions.

Disciple Builder: The foundation of the rest of the disciple's Christian life is his personal relationship with Jesus. Therefore, it is important to go through content slowly enough for him to apply the truths he is learning. It is tempting to study material (information) and then go on to the next topic without waiting for God the Holy Spirit to use time and circumstances to make the truths real in daily life.

Regarding teaching on the Holy Spirit, the emphasis here should be on the role of the Spirit (as the source of power, the fruit of the Spirit, etc.) in the believer's growth process, not on the spiritual gifts.

Cultivates Relationships with God and Christians (A)
Disciple:

13a   Is regularly involved with Christian activities: accepts small tasks within the body, seeks fellowship with Christians.

13b   Is committed to a small group Bible study, open to correction.

13c   Is developing a growing relationship with Jesus: is cultivating a daily quiet time (prayer, Bible study, Scripture memory, etc.), is seeking to walk obediently with Christ daily, is talking with others about Jesus and is growing in sensitivity to sin.

13d   Is developing an awareness of own emotional issues and is willing to work on them.

Disciple Builder: The definition of "committed" here means to attend faithfully, complete brief homework assignments and meet occasionally with the leader. Commitment at the beginning of the small group may be less than this; however, the disciple should be growing toward this commitment. At this point in the disciple's growth, the leader should be available to answer questions and help with faith steps, but not crowd the disciple or try to force growth. Be careful not to require (expect) too much commitment too soon. Your level of commitment to the disciple needs to reflect the disciple's level of commitment.

As a disciple builder, realize that disciples do not all grow at the same rate. Based on emotional maturity, personality and personal circumstances, growth rates will vary. Learn to be comfortable with (and sensitive to) the fact that growth in an individual, and therefore in a group, will not be orderly nor perfectly predictable. Guidelines presented here are just that – guidelines, not rigid standards.

You know that a disciple is becoming a "Ministry Trainee" (Phase III: Equipping for Ministry) when he exhibits the traits and habits listed in "A" (Accountability) consistently. These are evidence of a strong personal relationship with Christ, which is the critical foundational need at this point. To hurry the development of this relationship is a mistake. Remember that Christlike character as well as conduct is the goal – not just doing the right things, but being a "virtuous" person and turning away from sin as a lifestyle.

Understanding and Growth (P) Disciple Builder prays:

14a   For disciple to understand who Jesus is, what He has done and how to walk with Him, and to begin to meet with Christ in a daily quiet time (John 6:44; Ephesians 1:18-22).

14b   For personal needs in disciple's life, for disciple's growth in dependence on Jesus to meet personal needs, to see Jesus work in day-to-day life.

14c   For disciple to continue to turn from old lifestyle, establish new habits, experience Christian fellowship, develop a seriousness about God's will and Word.

14d   For disciple to develop healthy ways of dealing with emotions and getting needs met.

Involvement in Body of Christ (S) Disciple:

15a   Is allowed to observe leader in relationship with God and in ministry situations; disciple meets with leader periodically.

15b Is asked to help with tasks (especially physical tasks, not tasks that require spiritual experience and maturity). Is asked to get involved in the body of Christ.

15c Attends small group Bible study and/or a *Restoring Your Heart* group (if applicable).

Phase III
Equipping for Ministry

Mentoring (R) Disciple Builder:

16a   Chooses a select, open group of disciples. New people may be added, but group membership is by invitation only. Group is used as a filtering process to determine who should be appointed leaders later.

16b   Meets regularly with the disciple to apply basic ministry skill material (especially "P"—Participation of OPSI), to develop a good personal relationship and to hold each other accountable for personal and spiritual goals.

16c   Encourages disciple to establish casual friendships with unbelievers and to grow in commitment to other believers (in social situations, service activities, projects, etc.).

16d   Encourages disciple to learn relational principles and skills.

Law and Grace (C) Disciple Builder:

17a   Trains disciple in basic ministry skills: evangelism, testimony preparation, inductive Bible study, time management and healthy relationships.

17b   Teaches disciple about nature of God's Kingdom: benefits of Christ's redemptive work (deliverance from disease, demons and death, forgiveness of sin, justification by faith and freedom from the law), the power and leadership of Holy Spirit, spiritual warfare and walking by grace (not under law).

17c   Teaches disciple the vision of discipleship. Emphasizes balance between evangelism and service, adapting the Gospel, and the priority of ministry (balance).

17d   Teaches disciple how to develop healthy relationships.

Disciple Builder: Remember that the truth Christ taught His disciples often unfolded in stages throughout the growth process. This is true in the area of spiritual warfare. At the Ministry Trainee level (Phase III: Equipping for Ministry), you need to focus on the fact that there are opposing forces in our world, the sources of those forces, the supremacy of Christ in the warfare and the weapons of warfare believers have.

Becomes Ministry-Minded (A) Disciple:

18a   Begins to minister to those around him: takes responsibility for tasks within the ministry ("P"—Participation—part of OPSI) and shares Christ with others (including testimony and follow-up).

18b   Actively takes a stand for the Gospel by sharing his faith and by being identified with Christians.

18c   Makes ministry a priority: develops Christian friends to minister with, is accountable to leader (ministry trainer), is a faithful member of group designed to teach ministry skills and develops a vision for discipleship.

18d   Develops healthy relationships and proper boundaries in ministry endeavors.

Disciple Builder: Part of the purpose of taking responsibility for tasks within the ministry is to give the disciple an opportunity to try different areas of ministry to discover his spiritual gifts. The phrase "being identified with Christians" in 18b does not refer to the fact that a disciple needs to be publicly identified with Christ through baptism. (Ideally, this faith step already was taken when the disciple became a Christian.) It does refer to the disciple actively taking a stand for the Gospel by sharing his faith, giving a personal testimony, being identified with a Christian ministry, etc.

When a disciple understands how to develop healthy relationships, he does not force the Gospel on others and does not try to manipulate a response to the Gospel. He also knows how to maintain healthy boundaries in ministry so he doesn't allow others to take advantage of his time and resources.

When a disciple exhibits the elements listed above in "A" (Accountability), he is showing evidence of being ready to be appointed as a "New Leader" (Phase IV: Developing New Leaders). As before, remember that growth is more than just doing activities. In addition to doing the right activities, there needs to be growth in godly character. In this Phase, there is an emphasis on having a correct assessment of and perspective on the spiritual world.

Courage and Provision (P) Disciple Builder prays:

19a   That disciple sees the priority of ministry, grows in desire for ministry, and has opportunities to minister and grow in commitment to the body (Luke 5:8-10).

19b   That disciple understands Jesus' power to forgive (Luke 5:16-26).

19c   That there will be an open door for Gospel, that disciple will develop a burden for the lost and become bold in his witness.

19d   That disciple understands that having healthy relationships is a priority if he is to be effective in ministry.

Opportunity to Serve and Witness (S) Disciple:

20a   Accepts small challenges in ministry (Does "P"—Participation—part of OPSI).

20b   Is in a Ministry Training group.

20c   Attends a short-term mission project.

20d   Learns about ministry relationships from a variety of ministry opportunities.

Phase IV
Developing New Leaders

Part A — Appointing New Leaders

Training (R) Disciple Builder:

21a   Chooses select, closed group of disciples (for leadership group).

21b   Encourages strong commitments among this group of disciples.

21c   Meets regularly with disciple and continues to be a model for him.

Disciple Builder: Choosing leaders is a critical event in the life of a group as well as in the lives of disciples. Be sure to apply biblical qualifications — especially godly character -- as you evaluate (qualities in the Sermon on the Mount). Jesus spent all night in prayer before choosing the Twelve. Thus, we need to follow His example and seek God diligently and humbly when choosing leaders.

There are some common mistakes to avoid when appointing leaders. First, do not appoint people as leaders before they have had enough time and opportunity to demonstrate faithfulness. The leader needs to observe and interact with the disciple over time. On the other hand, do not wait too long to give developing leaders responsibilities. We all grow by being challenged! Obviously, a balance is needed: prayer and careful discernment are necessary. Also, if there are no people to lead, do not appoint leaders.

Leadership Principles: Character, Authority (C) Disciple Builder:

22a Teaches Sermon on the Mount. Includes topics such as Christian character, ethical conduct, meaning of heart obedience, true worship, eternal perspective on issues in culture, and parables of the Kingdom (Matthew 13).

22b Teaches Parables of the Kingdom including extending the kingdom to others, conflict with Satan's kingdom (spiritual warfare), and growth of the Kingdom.

22c Teaches about discipleship in the family, spiritual gifts, discipleship philosophy (an overview), and ministry to the hurting (healing).

Disciple Builder: The concept of the "Kingdom" and believers as "Kingdom people" is a theme at this point and should be emphasized. Disciples should be encouraged to try different ministry situations with the goal of discovering their spiritual gifts. New leaders should be learning to identify emotional problems and how to help others begin to heal.

Assumes Leadership Responsibilities (A) Disciple:

23a Has a personal ministry ("S"—Supervision—of OPSI): assumes responsibility and leadership in ministry, grows in his ability to study the Bible (inductive Bible study and special literature like Parables), and faithfully shares the Gospel.

23b Has a consistent walk with God, exhibits godly character (Sermon on the Mount) and grows in dependence on God.

23c Takes bold stands on spiritual and moral issues.

Disciple Builder: Realize that your disciple, a new leader, has needs and areas to continue to grow in and does not have experience to draw from. Therefore you may need to drop back to the "P" phase of OPSI in an area to meet a need he has. When a disciple exhibits the elements listed above in "A" (Accountability), he is showing evidence of being ready to move on to the stage of Phase IV: Developing New Leaders – Part B. Again, the emphasis is not on living the Christian life perfectly, but on general growth progressing toward Christlike maturity.

Perspective and Wisdom (P) Disciple Builder prays:

24a   For discernment in selection of new leaders.

24b   For disciples (new leaders) to have an effective ministry to others. Prays that there are new disciples for new leaders to lead, that disciples are able to see potential in younger believers, and that disciples are strengthened by the Holy Spirit.

24c   For disciples to continue to grow in godly character, to be obedient to the principles in Sermon on Mount, and to be protected from the evil one (especially from spiritual pride).

Appointment to Leadership Roles (S) Disciple:

25a   Participates in leadership group (retreats, meetings, etc.) and in mission projects (short-term, domestic and overseas).

25b   Meets regularly with leader for accountability, encouragement and instruction.

25c   Has a personal ministry ("S"—Supervision—of OPSI) and provides leadership in the movement.

Part B — Focusing on Eternal Things

Encouraging (R) Disciple Builder:

26a   Continues with select, closed group chosen in Phase IV-A, and builds intimate relationships.

26b   Models transparency.

26c   Makes sure that disciple has a personal ministry with believers being equipped for ministry ("S"—Supervision—of OPSI).

Eternal Perspective (C) Disciple Builder:

27a   Teaches disciples to re-evaluate their world view: eternal values are superior to temporal ones (Philippians 1:12-14,18). This includes racial and cross-cultural issues, materialism, legalism, etc.

27b   Teaches about Christ's sufficiency: His provision enables us to do whatever He demands. Victory in spiritual battle comes only by the Holy Spirit.

27c   Teaches about sovereignty of God: how to follow divine authority over human tradition, about biblical authority and how it should be administered, and about the openness of the kingdom to all (universal nature of the church).

27d   Teaches about having realistic biblical expectations for Christian growth and development. Teaches about how to "sort out good and bad." (That is, teaches disciple how to emotionally live with the simultaneous existence of good and bad in himself, in others and in our world.)

Disciple Builder: The theme of "eternal vs. temporal" values affects many areas of a disciple's life in addition to the ones listed in 27a. The general principle is that daily life is filled with choices – how to spend money, where to live, where to work, etc. – and eternal values need to be the guide for decision-making rather that temporal ones.

Regarding 27d: included here is a theology of suffering. How does a Christian deal with hard times, illnesses, disappointments, failure, etc.? Too often, Christian culture does not address these issues, and thus seems to imply that they do not exist for the Christian. A related issue is the fact that as Christians we live in a state of "now but not yet" – the kingdom has come on earth through and in us, and yet, at the same time, the kingdom is still in the future.

Adjusts Expectations (A) Disciple:

28a   Rejects worldly values and embraces eternal values.

28b   Submits to biblical authorities and to Word of God (over the word of men).

28c   Lives in a way that reflects God's grace and obedience rather than a rewards/punishment mind-set.

28d   Has realistic view of the world and himself as being both good and bad. Is able to give himself and others grace.

Disciple Builder: When a disciple exhibits the elements listed above in "A" (Accountability), he is showing evidence of being ready to move on to the stage of Phase V: Developing Mature Leaders – Part A. The disciple continues to have a ministry.

Endurance (P) Disciple Builder prays:

29a   That disciple will be discerning and live for eternal values.

29b   That disciple will see the glorified Christ – His authority on earth and in heaven.

29c   That disciple will have understanding in spiritual battles.

29d   That disciple has an accurate view of God, self and others.

Acceptance of Difficult Assignments (S) Disciple:

30a   Participates in leadership group (retreats, meetings, etc.) and in mission projects (short-term, domestic and overseas).

30b   Meets regularly with the leader for accountability, encouragement and instruction.

30c   Participates in evangelistic outreaches to new classes of people.

Disciple Builder: It is important that content in this section be taught in an atmosphere of grace and encouragement. Many of the topics deal with principles of lifestyle (how much is enough, living a simple life, etc.), and an improper emphasis on these topics can develop. Some people tend to drift toward the extreme of asceticism in which there is a belief that it is "more spiritual" to do without and to judge people who don't agree. Be sensitive to this danger.

Phase V
Developing Mature Leaders

Part A—Delegating New Responsibilities

Delegating (R) Disciple Builder:

31a   Continues with select, closed group chosen in Phase IV-A, and continues to build intimate relationships.

31b   Models suffering love to disciples (leadership team).

31c   Also, models loyalty and faithfulness to disciples (leadership team).

Team Ministry (C) Disciple Builder:

32a   Models and teaches: unity and harmony in the body of Christ; discipline in the body of Christ; reconciliation of brother in sin; and trust in Christ to work in other members of the body (Romans 14).

32b   Models and teaches how to deal with conflicts outside the body regarding false religions and opposition from Christians outside the group.

32c   Teaches team leadership and delegation of responsibility, and develops ministries related to spiritual gifts and calling.

Fosters Unity (A) Disciple:

33a   Willingly forgives an offending brother.

33b   Trusts God to work through others in the midst of disagreements.

33c   Submits to difficult authorities without compromising truth.

33d   Helps give leadership to the overall ministry and to a specialized ministry related to gifting.

Disciple Builder: When disciples exhibit the elements listed above in "A" (Accountability), they are showing evidence of being ready to move on to the stage of Phase V: Developing Mature Leaders – Part B. Other qualities that will be evident are an ability to delegate (trust God to work in and through others), to confront sin and to grow in unselfishness.

Unity in Diversity (P) Disciple Builder prays:

34a   That disciple will have a burden for intercessory prayer.

34b   That disciple will deal with confrontation in the body in a biblical way (Matthew 18:15-21).

34c   That disciple will be bold and be protected from Satan's attacks and criticism.

34d   That disciple will remain humble and learn to serve those he is leading

Ability to Work with Other Leaders (S) Disciple:

35a   Participates in the leadership group (retreats, meetings, etc.).

35b   Meets regularly with the leader for accountability, encouragement and instruction.

35c   Provides leadership in the overall movement.

Disciple Builder: A pitfall at this point is to fail to give the mature leader increasing responsibility and decision-making authority. A disciple needs to be operating relatively independently in his ministry with occasional check-in points for accountability and advice. In contrast, the personal relationship with the disciple deepens and grows in commitment.

Part B—Casting a World Vision

Commissioning (R) Disciple Builder:

36a Continues with select, closed group. Helps them build intimate relationships. Has disciples participate on a leadership team.

36b Is sure that disciple's relationship with him is primarily a peer relationship.

36c Perseveres in difficult relationships.

Resurrection Power in Daily Life (C) Disciple Builder:

37a Teaches all-sufficiency of Christ as He ministered and rested in the power of the Spirit rather than in the flesh. Also teaches about spiritual warfare and dependent prayer.

37b Teaches and models sacrificial nature of leadership: throne perspective (i.e., all things are ours, so give up the world) and love, as the mark of the Christian.

37c Teaches about developing a world vision and about personal responsibility to spread the gospel.

Disciple Builder: You as the leader may need to help the disciple articulate specific goals for ministry.

Show Sacrificial Love to Reach the World (A) Disciple:

38a   Trusts and rests in the Spirit alone in spite of circumstances. Consistently desires to show suffering love.

38b   Lives life characterized by dependent prayer.

38c   Has a ministry vision and a world vision.

Disciple Builder: It is important to help the disciple avoid the danger of self-confident professionalism, i.e., trusting abilities, especially ministry abilities, instead of God.

Sacrificial Love (P) Disciple Builder prays:

39a   That disciple understands that ministry can be carried out only in the power of the Holy Spirit.

39b   That Holy Spirit works in lives as Gospel is proclaimed.

39c   That disciple and his ministry are protected from power of Satan.

Acceptance of Worldwide Challenge (S) Disciple:

40a   Takes leadership in the movement.

40b   Functions independently from leader.

40c   Attends and/or organizes prayer meetings for empowering disciples to be Christ's witnesses.

Notes

Introduction

1. Chaves, Mark. 2011. The Decline of American Religion? (ARDA Guiding Paper Series). State College, PA: The Association of Religion Data Archives at The Pennsylvania State University, from http://www.thearda.com/rrh/papers/guidingpapers.asp.

2. Dr. Richard J. Krejcir, "Statistics on Pastors," *Into Thy Word Archive*, 2007, http://www.intothyword.org/apps/articles/?articleid=36562

3. John Ortberg, *The Life You Always Wanted* (Grand Rapids, MI: Zondervan, 1997), 32.

4. Ibid, p.33

5. "Are Christians More Like Jesus or More Like Pharisees?", *Barna Group*, 2013, https://www.barna.org/culture-articles/611-new-barna-study-explores-trends-among-american-donors

Chapter 1. The Priority and Benefits of Maturity

6. The often quoted phrase: *"Not until I went into the churches of America and heard her pulpits flame with righteousness did I understand the secret of her genius and power. America is great because she is good, and*

if America ever ceases to be good, she will cease to be great." is often attributed to Alexis de Toqueville in *Democracy in America.* (The quote actually originated in a campaign speech by Dwight Eisenhower in 1952, who cited the source as *"a wise philosopher [who] came to this country."*) However, the idea of a robust spirituality being a foundation stone for America was a core tenant of Toqueville's work since he cited the Puritan influence as a critical factor in the development of the young republic. Jesus was the King-Statesman who enabled the Christian Founding Fathers to be "salt and light" in this nation.

7.   Dallas Willard, *The Divine Conspiracy: Rediscovering Our Hidden Life in God* (New York, NY: Harper San Francisco, 1998), Introduction xv.

8.   http://www.gallup.com/poll/159548/identify-christian.aspx

9.   http://thegospelcoalition.org/blogs/tgc/2012/09/25/factchecker-divorce-rate-among-christians/

10. Chaves, Mark. 2011. The Decline of American Religion? (ARDA Guiding Paper Series). State College, PA: The Association of Religion Data Archives at The Pennsylvania State University, from http://www.thearda.com/rrh/papers/guidingpapers.asp.

11. *"I think highly of the epistle of James, and regard it as valuable although it was rejected in early days. It does not expound human doctrines, but lays much emphasis on God's law. ...I do not hold it to be of apostolic authorship."* Martin Luther, as quoted by William Barclay, *The Daily Study Bible Series, The Letters of James and Peter, Revised Edition* (Louisville, KY: Westminster John Knox Press, 1976), 7.

12. "Few modern Christians can read the works of the Reformers and doubt that what was happening in the Reformation was a genuine work of spiritual renewal, as well as a traumatic adjustment of doctrines, practices and systems of political control within Western Christianity. New spiritual life broke out in the church wherever Luther's doctrine penetrated. There were, however, limits to its pen-

etration. It captured intellectual and spiritual leaders and their territories, but it did not always revive the great masses of the laity in any depth and number.

Subsequent generations of Protestants were capable of turning Luther's teaching into dead orthodoxy, and this seems to have happened especially in the Lutheran sector. Here a one-sided emphasis on justification, along with the resulting neglect of sanctification and the uses of the law, often produced what Bonhoeffer has bitingly called "cheap grace." Luther had warned against this abuse of his doctrine, and Calvin had included in his Institutes a carefully balanced treatment of sanctification. But by the end of the sixteenth century, Protestants in both the Lutheran and Reformed spheres were referring to the "half-reformation" which had reformed their doctrines but not their lives, and were seeking for a new revitalization of the church.

The pre-Pietism of Johann Arndt and the early Puritanism which took hold in England, Holland and America retained the reformation emphasis on sanctification and particularly regeneration, the spiritual rebirth of the converted Christian. These two movements, Puritanism and Pietism, were undoubtedly powerful religious awakenings which penetrated the church extensively, reaching both leaders and lay people." Richard Lovelace, *Dynamics of Spiritual Life: An Evangelical Theology of Renewal* (Downers Grove, IL: Intervarsity Press, 1980), 34-35.

13. John Piper, *God is the Gospel* (Wheaton, IL: Crossway Books, 2005), 45.

14. Alister McGrath, *Spirituality in An Age of Change: Re-discovering the Spirit of the Reformers* (Grand Rapids: Zondervan Publishing House, 1994), 9.

15. John Piper, *The Dangerous Duty of Delight: The Glorified God and the Satisfied Soul* (Sisters, OR: Multnomah, 2001), 78.

16. John Burke, *No Perfect People Allowed* (Grand Rapids, MI: Zondervan, 2005), 69-70.

17. Jonathan Dodson, *Gospel Centered Discipleship* (Wheaton, IL: Crossway, 2012), 17.

Chapter 2. What Is Maturity?

18. Irenaus of Lyons: *A Treatise Against the Heresies* (Book 4: Chapter 20). The phrase: *"Gloria Dei est vivens homo"* (Lat.) is probably better translated *"the glory of God is a living man"* which supports the point we make in this section. Unfortunately, the often quoted (more popular) translation: *"the glory of God is man fully alive"* is sometimes used as an apologetic for the modern self-fulfillment movement. When read in context, the statement (in my estimation) is clearly an argument for the glory of God revealed in and through Jesus Christ and reflected in the people who behold Him (and become like Him) through the Gospel. (cf. II Cor. 4:4-6)

19. Section H1: "Christian Maturing: Definition," *The Nottingham Statement*

20. Dr. J.I. Packer, *Rediscovering Holiness* (Ann Arbor, MI: Servant Publications, 1992), 28.

21. John Piper, *God is the Gospel* (Wheaton, IL: Crossway Books, 2005), 16.

22. Jerry Bridges, *The Practice of Godliness* (Colorado Springs, CO: NavPress, 1983, 1986), 15.

23. Dallas Willard, *The Divine Conspiracy: Rediscovering Our Hidden Life in God* (New York, NY: Harper San Francisco, 1998), Introduction xiii.

24. An unsubstantiated quote by American Jurist Oliver Wendell Holmes, Jr. (1841-1935) who may have paraphrased his father: Oliver Wendell Holmes, Sr. (1809-1894). Regardless of the source, it's often quoted to illustrate this point. (ref. *wikiquote.org, goodreads.com, businesssimplification.com, et al*)

Chapter 3. Five Progressive Phases of Maturity

25. Robert Coleman, *The Master Plan of Evangelism* (Ada, MI: Revell, 1964; reprint ed. 2010), 21

26. *The WebBible Encyclopedia - Jesus: The Years of Jesus Christ's Ministry* (christiananswers.net)

27. http://www.disciplebuilding.org/product-category/laying-foundations-phase-2/

28. The term *Apostle* (literally: "sent one") has a unique meaning and usage when it refers to the commissioning of The Twelve and others (such as Paul, Barnabas, et al) who were the formative, foundational establishers of the Church (2 Cor. 12:11-12). This type of Apostleship, or proximity to an Apostle as in the case of Luke, was one of the markers for the acceptance of their writing into the Scriptural canon. The gift of apostleship (1 Cor. 12:28 and Ephesians 4) seems to refer to those who had the gift of being a church planter, though not in the same sense as the original Apostles, and as such applies throughout the Church age. Not every church leader (overseer/elder) has the gift of apostleship. But all leaders need to be equipped and authority conveyed to them through the already established leadership hierarchy (the laying on of hands). This is the affirmation of the church that these leaders have been trained and examined in matters of doctrine, character, mission, etc. and thus retain spiritual authority to carry out their calling.

Chapter 4. Removing Hindrances to Maturity

29. Jack Larson, *The 2820 Video Conference* (Fayetteville, GA: WDA, 2006), Session #3: *How Emotional Problems Develop.*

Chapter 5. Maturity: The Church is God's "Plan A"

30. Wayne Blank, "Parakletos", *Daily Bible Study,* *www.keyway.ca/htm2001/20010727.htm*

Chapter 6. "And When the Chief Shepherd Appears..."

31. Dr. Richard J. Krejcir, "Statistics on Pastors," *Into Thy Word Archive,* 2007,

http://www.intothyword.org/apps/articles/?articleid=36562

Acknowledgements

I find it very difficult to appropriately acknowledge and thank all the people who have contributed to the completion of this project. Collaboration and unity are always at the heart of any significant and pivotal work of God. I'm not sure if this work qualifies as "significant and pivotal," but the collegial spirit of these friends and colleagues inspired me to launch and sustained me to finish this book. I am indeed grateful. Regardless of its impact, I offer my deep thanks to each one. Blessings!

In a project like this, success is in the details. Thanks to Buddy Eades, Nila Duffitt, Margaret Garner, David Parfitt and Linda Dukes for performing the painstaking duty of managing the tedium.

When it comes to my skills as a writer, I've had to face the fact that I'm not very good, but I sure am slow. Thanks to my editor, Marti Pieper, who patiently corrected run-on-sentences, pedantic style, bad grammar, and punctuation from Mars.

For decades, the staff members of Worldwide Discipleship Association (WDA) have worked tirelessly to "present people mature in Christ." They are disciple builders who have life-researched and implemented the growth principles in this book. I know these approaches work because these people have joined me in employing them to help others grow. Many have moved on to other leadership roles, but I still have the privilege of working alongside some of them. I offer a note of gratitude to the members of the WDA Curriculum Team and especially to Jack Larson, Margaret Garner, and David Parfitt.

Satan will fiercely oppose any work of worth in the Kingdom of God. Resisting the devil requires wise leadership. We must stand in unity with the armor of God in place, praying diligently and following the Spirit faithfully. I've been blessed with a Board of Directors composed of leaders of this caliber. The WDA band of warriors, led by Ross Greene and Dan Horne, has helped us navigate rough seas and steer a path that has positioned this organization to "serve the Church worldwide by teaching people to disciple others." To all the board members and their spouses, past and present, I owe a huge measure of gratitude. Your unselfish service, wisdom and care has guided WDA through the decades, and God has used you in a mighty way.

Years ago, I abandoned plans to attend an Ivy League law school to accept a ministry position that offered no guaranteed salary. Many predicted it wouldn't last long, and I would soon be forced to "get a real job." Working at WDA has never been a real job in the sense of being mundane and predictable, but it has brought great fulfillment, and I hope to continue for many years to come. It has also required faith, but I've had a corps of committed ministry partners whose faithful prayers and sacrificial giving have kept me employed. Thank you, dear friends. I long for the Day when the Father reveals your treasure in heaven.

When trying to capture the process of growth to maturity, one must stand on the shoulders of ministry giants. And when it comes to practical discipleship, many notable contributors have provided wisdom and insight. I committed my life to Christ in 1972 while listening to the re-broadcast of Billy Graham's 1968 Chicago Crusade. I also appreciate the writings and example of Robert Coleman, Daws Trotman, Dallas Willard, Howard Hendricks, Bill Bright, J. I. Packer, John Piper, Tim Keller, and many others who helped forge my spiritual development and shape my thinking. Some of these leaders are now with Christ. All are part of a generation that helped launch and steer the modern discipleship movement and remain shining stars in its firmament.

Carl Wilson, WDA's founding president, influenced me as no other. His unswerving commitment to classic, orthodox theology and his research of the ministry of our Lord as a paradigm for leadership development helped frame the R-CAPS architecture explained in this book. I'll always be grateful for his patience with my youth and immaturity. His vision, wisdom, and courage are exceptional gifts to the Church.

Every process must have a proving ground, a place where theory becomes practice, and where "Why don't we try this?" becomes a reproducible program. To the courageous staff and lay leaders at New Hope Baptist Church in Fayetteville, Georgia, I offer my profound thanks. A special thank you goes to Pastor Rhys Stenner, who left Great Britain to shepherd God's flock in America. You're a great expositor, leader, and pioneer, and an even better friend. Thanks also to Dr. Tim Woodruff, who remembers using mimeographs to communicate many of the principles in this book while an undergraduate at the University of Georgia. Your wisdom and tenacity have repeatedly proven the point that nothing is more practical than a good theory. Woody Johnson, I especially appreciate that you had the vision and wisdom to see the future, and the faith and courage to sacrificially serve and make it a reality. And my gratitude also goes out to Dr. Hugh Kirby, who for decades has passionately communicated the principles and practices of Life Coaching, but is primarily a man everyone wants to follow. Relationships are your heart and your legacy.

Finally, I'm so very grateful to my wife, Linda, my children, their spouses, and my grandchildren. They all know how much I need to mature. Too often, they drew the short straw of my time and energy while I pursued the false god of career success and struggled to heal from past pain. The maturity of my grown children amazes me. I know their growth and development is more a product of God's grace and faithfulness than my application of this book's principles. Linda, you've walked with me for most of life and participated fully in fleshing out this discipleship strategy. Your help and perspective have been invaluable. Thank you for cheering me on while reading, editing, and re-reading this manuscript to help finalize this project. You've prayed for us all to grow while fasting and waiting for God to work His grace. You're our emotional anchor and a true picture of Christlikeness. There aren't enough words to convey my gratitude or my love.

I'm sorry it's taken me so long to have my heart restored enough to write these words. But I rejoice that "He who began a good work in us" will finish it as well. I pray my experience offers some wisdom for others to glean. Through His Spirit, by His grace, and for His glory, I purpose never to stop working on my issues nor cease combating Satan's lies but to press on and grow up into Christ. One day, I'll make it home to the presence of our Father and become completely transformed into the image of the Son. God be praised!

About the Author

Robert D. (Bob) Dukes is the President and Executive Director of Worldwide Discipleship Association headquartered in Fayetteville, Georgia.

Bob has been with WDA since it was founded in 1974. Prior to becoming WDA's 2nd President in 1997, he served as Campus Director at The University of Tennessee, National Campus Director, and Executive Director/Vice-President. He is the author/co-author of many educational publications and articles including: *Disciple Building: A Biblical Framework; Disciple Building: A Practical Strategy; Small Groups Manual;* and *Life Coaching Manual.* He serves as a founding member of The Steering Committee for The Pierce Center for Disciple Building at Gordon-Conwell Theological Seminary in Boston, MA.

Bob graduated from Columbia University in New York and attended Reformed Theological Seminary. He was awarded several honorary athletic and academic honors including Columbia's prestigious "1917 Football Cup." He was a finalist for The Rhodes Scholarship, selected as an "Outstanding Young Man of the Year" by The International Jaycees, and inducted into The East Tennessee Football Hall of Fame.

Bob and his wife, Linda, reside in Fayetteville, GA and have five children and many grandchildren.

For more information on Worldwide Discipleship Association, visit:
http://www.disciplebuilding.org

Made in the USA
San Bernardino, CA
21 January 2017